CUSTOMERS RUN YOUR COMPANY:

They Pay The Bills !

Second Edition:1991

Michale J. Bandley
Elizabeth I. Kearney
KEARNEY/BANDLEY ENTERPRISES

Barbra Anderson
Mary Jo Tellin
SEARCH FOR EXCELLENCE, INC.

Sterling Press
563 Washington Blvd.
Marina del Rey, CA 90202

I.S.B.N. 0-942501-06-3

Printed in the United States of America
by Community Press, Provo, Utah
First Printing, 1990

Layout/typesetting by Analee H. Perica
Los Angeles, California

COMMENTS TO NOTE

"Amid all the rhetoric about customer service, its refreshing to find someone to tell us what to do to make sure our business is customer focused. This is, no doubt, the central issue in company survival in the international market, and this book presents the central methods in a very usable format."

Joel W. Warner
Vice President--Human Resources
CSX Transportation

"This book is 'right on target' for companies that want to be successful in the 90's. Everyone in your organization from the top down must get closer to their primary source of revenue--the customer! Follow the rules in this book, and you will have no problem keeping old customers and collecting new ones."

J.A. Burton
Director, Applications Development
Dow Plastics

"Reading CUSTOMERS RUN YOUR BUSINESS: THEY PAY THE BILLS is like winning a game. It gives you the preparation, the tools, and the great feeling that lets you know you are the best you can be!!

Ted Dawson
Nationally Known Sportscaster
CBS Affiliate

ACKNOWLEDGEMENT

We would like to express our thanks to Analee Perica and Darrell Weireter whose help, encouragement, and support have added so much to this project.

FOREWORD

There's a poster on a wall in my office entitled, "Why Customers Leave"

1% die
3% move
5% buy from friends
9% prefer the competition
14% judge all like businesses due to one bad encounter
68% leave because of indifference, rudeness, or lack of service from an employee.

That message, though stark, in essence confirms the philosophy of this book: "Businesses that are customer-service driven survive and thrive; those that are not—do not!!"

Poor customer service is related to the very basics of business sense, especially when we consider that elemental part of every business—the Organization Chart:

President

Vice President Sales — VP — VP — VP
Sales Manager
Salesperson
Customer

Where is the customer? Last!! Thus, there is an internal focus. A progressive and excellent VP in my company once said—and believes and preaches—"Let us strive for customer excellence, not internal perfection."

A better Organization Chart would be the reverse of the one above, and the customer would come first. Doesn't this reflect how information should flow—market trends, influences, competitive information, effectiveness of deliveries, invoices, sales service, order entry, and customer satisfaction!! Effective feedback comes from the top down, and the top of any business should be the customer.

When the flow of information comes from the customer, it costs less, resources are applied to real customer needs, and the customer-driven company takes in more revenue with fewer costs. Isn't that the way it should be?

A final note—good customer service varies for every person within the firm. For example, in Industrial Sales:

- good customer service makes the operator on the floor's job easier
- good customer service helps the product superintendent get quality product out the door on schedule
- good customer service gives the engineer a simpler process with easier controls
- and good customer service gives increased profits to the President/Owner.

Customer service—lip service or good service? You tell me!

Howard G. Seebach
Dupont

PREFACE

The implementation of the principles of successful customer service sets successful companies apart from others, and the readers of this book will find specific guidelines and suggestions for putting these principles into practice in their company or organization.

Over the years I have found that success reflects, sometimes without the person even realizing it, a well-developed ability to relate to others, recognize and respond to their needs, and a willingness to modify and change when necessary. The authors of this book have taken this concept and developed strategies that can be applied and utilized by the readers—strategies that can make a major difference because they put the customer first.

The information is presented in an interesting, even entertaining, way, and, although theory is not ignored, it is coupled with practicality and tips that can be put to immediate use. Their first co-authored book, EVERYONE IS A CUSTOMER, stressed the idea that everyone we encounter is a customer of ideas, products, or services. This book takes this concept to its logical conclusion—the major marketshare will go to those organizations and companies that are truly service-driven. Companies in trouble tend to exacerbate their present situation by avoiding the needs of their customers and forgetting what made the company originally successful. It is a difficult mind set to make customer service the number one priority, but those companies that create the ubiquitous sense of customer satisfaction in their firms will rise to the top of their industry scale.

Be passionate about quality, lead in information technology, go international, innovate, emphasize improvement, and thrive on change, but never forget who your customer is and how to resolve his needs.

Russell H. Schreck
President/CEO
Craig Consumer
Electronics

TABLE OF CONTENTS

1

THE CUSTOMER REVOLT

**"In today's competitive marketplace,
the customer decides
who wins and who loses."**

**John Humphrey, Chairman
The Forum Corporation**

The first troops in the lettuce war may really have been the vanguard of the customer revolt. The power of disenchanted buyers was all too evident some years back when they decided to boycott lettuce until they achieved their goal—a lower price. It did not take long for producers to realize that they were not in the power position, the consumers were. This same message has been repeated a number of times in the last 10 to 15 years, and we know what an organized boycott of consumers can do.

This power has shifted somewhat and the fear of what can happen when such a revolt occurs and the knowledge that it can occur has become a powerful tool in the marketplace. Add this knowledge to the increasing awareness levels of John and Jane Q. Public. The media keeps them informed when companies mismanage. Chrysler learned this when the media announced that it had sold demonstration models as new cars. Lee Iacocca faced the public head-on and apologized in a full page ad run nationally. The media also alerts the public when there is danger to health or limb. Companies that respond quickly and let the public know that it really does come first survive crises and sometimes even gain from them because of the positive publicity generated by their obvious practice of putting the customer first. Johnson and Johnson came through the Tylenol crisis in good shape because it acted—and let the world know it acted—with the welfare of the customer in mind.

When this attitude is not present or is not seen as being present, public wrath becomes a powerful, profit-destroying force. Such was the case in early 1989 when an unfortunate oil spill in Alaska brought Exxon policies to the attention of the world. The company response was viewed negatively—the clean-up plan was seen as unclear and many questioned the company's level of concern for the consequences of one of history's worst spills. Whether there was a lack of concern or an inadequate plan is immaterial, the fact that perception held that to be true is what really led to the customer anger and revolt which was shown by thousands of torn up credit cards being returned to Exxon's corporate offices.

If customer statistics are considered, then the consequences of that spill go far beyond what is visible dissatisfaction. Remember

- Customer purchases are largely based upon input and advice from others.

- The average business doesn't hear from 96% of the unhappy customers (in light of that statistic, we know that many who didn't take overt action and tear up and mail back the card will just drive past Exxon stations and silently voice their disapproval.)

- For every one complaint at headquarters, 26 go unreported.

- 65% to 90% of non-complaining customers with a problem will not buy from you again.

- A customer with a bad experience will tell as many as 11 other people.

- 13% will tell 20 people or more!

- Marketing data indicates that it costs five times as much to get a new customer as it does to keep an existing one.

What are the consequences of this customer revolt? **CHANGE!**

> **"The consumer of the Nineties will be the smartest customer we have ever dealt with...and respecting the smarts of the consumer is going to create major changes."**
>
> **Laurel Cutler, Vice Chairman**
> **FCB/Leber Katz**

We seem to be coming full circle. The cottage industry of the late 1800's had almost disappeared, even the local mom and pop stores were fading rapidly from view by the mid 1900's. Now national reports tell us that there is an astonishing growth of small businesses, including cottage industries which are taking many forms. Entrepreneurial based companies are accounting for the largest number of employees and collectively triggering major changes.

We all know someone who has started a business, and statistics show that the survival rate of those businesses is now in favor of the person accepting the challenge. In addition, many of these companies are women-owned. Add to this number the thousands who now work from home even though employed by large companies, and you have an important part of the workforce working out of the corporate structure—directly or indirectly.

Large companies controlled the marketplace for years, and the small companies struggled to stay alive, but now, according to an article that appeared in the *Wall Street Journal*, over half of the workforce is employed in companies with fewer than 100 employees. These companies can't afford to alienate even one customer or client, and they are not isolated from the consequences of their actions as are some of the larger corporations.

Because of the small firms' ability to act quickly when they spot a market need or respond quickly when they hear of a problem, they have been giving their "big brothers" a real run for the market share. The most successful large companies have responded by revising their approach. They have instituted feedback systems, hired mystery shoppers, sent quality control experts into the field to view and review their own practices, introduced incentive programs, and even provided for employee stock options and grants whose purpose is to make each employee feel that it is truly "his or her" company and that customer satisfaction is important to "his or her" personal welfare, too. Sears, whose pay rate has never been known as one of industry's highest, has maintained a relatively stable employee base for years, and when several employees were interviewed about this, they indicated that they really were part of the company—they owned stock in it. In other words, like the entrepreneur, they had a vested interest in seeing that the marketing and service plans worked. There is no doubt that Sears has also used the entrepreneur's approach to adjusting to the competition. In 1989, they did a media blitz and closed all stores for one day to reduce prices 50%—even their detractors were swayed by this action. They stressed that they would continue putting the customer first.

> **"Clearly, we have a premier niche in the marketplace because all our services are focused on client needs, and we recognize that delivery and superior client value are the only services we have to offer."**
>
> **R. Michael McCullough, Chairman**
> **Booz-Allen and Hamilton**

The 1970's and 1980's saw some other major changes—changes that were also triggered by customer revolt. Deregulation of the airlines, banks, trucking, the phone company all led to the growth of new companies and problems. This was the first time that customers were given a choice about their long distance phone service, and this choice has led to a highly competitive market, markedly different pricing, a push to woo customers by stressing the response time and improved customer service. In other words, the customers will have the last word because they always pick up the tab.

Some airlines have forgotten this. Airlines overbook, drop routes, leave late, have merged and remerged until the general public is frustrated and angry. The problems are still with us, but there is no doubt that many are striving to impress upon the flying public that "we are concerned about you." SAS ads play this theme over and over and reinforce it with vignettes of given events. For example,

> One 1988 advertisement told about a businessman in Europe who arrived at the airport without his ticket. The ticket agent invited him to go into the lounge while she took care of the problem. She dispatched a car to the hotel where he had left the ticket, had it picked up, brought back, and got him on the plane in time.

The point being made was that

- SAS cared
- was efficient in its handling of problems—even those they did not cause.
- took the extra steps needed to insure that each and every customer was given quality service and support.

Deregulation created many problems even while it was alerting the giants to the need to respond to those served, but the competition will continue to be rough for some time to come. To some extent the customer will be the winner, but will your company be able to respond to the intense competition?

Deregulation isn't the only thing altering the market structure. An article appearing in the *Wall Street Journal* on August 4, 1987, noted that there had been a decline in manufacturing and an increase in service jobs.

- Those services need to be available where and when the customer wants them.
- There needs to be greater interaction between the customer and the service provider.
- Fewer employees will be at each site so each will have to be customer-service oriented.

What will happen in your company as these changes take place. Each employee you have is literally your front line every time he/she interfaces directly, or even indirectly by billing, answering letters, or getting shipments out. What that person does can make or break that customer/company relationship. You can't afford to offer anything but the best—product or service.

For years, those working for the largest employer in the country—government, country, state, or local agencies, felt that they were not involved in customer relations. **How Untrue!** All we have to do now is look at the changing postal market to see that dissatisfaction has led to a sharp rise in competitive services. Service and speed, not cost, dictated the original shifts. And both are still major factors. More and more companies are turning to FAX machines to get their information to the other party quickly, more quickly than they could get it there by Express Mail or Federal Express. When this is coupled with the interfacing between computers and voice mail, it isn't hard to see why the U.S. Post Office instituted a customer service program several years ago.

It is time to ask yourself these questions:

- What do I offer that sets me apart from my competitors?
- What conditions within my company need to be handled in order to
  - improve service?
  - improve productivity?
  - improve profit?
- What steps am I willing and able to take to bring about the needed changes?

Write down your answers and then take notes as you go through the rest of this book. By the end of the book, you will have the information and techniques needed to take action—action that can make a major difference in your success level.

In fact, when you finish this book, you will have a blueprint for SUCCESS.

- **S** service driven
- **U** understanding customer needs
- **C** consistent service
- **C** corporate strategy planning
- **E** employee training
- **S** shopping for information
- **S** setting service goals that work.

With these elements in your success plan you will be able to move your company or organization from

- a production driven company to a customer driven one
- a solid company to a "world class" one
- a product focus to a customer focus
- a "how to" to "for you" attitude at all levels.

Marketing is going to have to change its focus. Consumers are going to take charge and may well reject manufacturers' compromises according to Laurel Cutler, vice-chairman of FCB/Leber Katz, a New York based advertising agency and vice-president of consumer affairs of Chrysler. She also notes that marketing is going to be even more important to business success in the future. "You're [going to look]for 20% of the people who are crazy about [the product] and can't live without it, and if 80% hate it, so what." She cited the marketing approach for Absolut, as an excellent example of what can be done with a successful advertising campaign in a market where the products themselves have little, if any, real difference. "Vodka is always the most interesting example, because by law it it tasteless and odorless. So what's the difference between one vodka and another? Nothing but marketing."

The baby boomers are now moving from an era of self-indulgence and are repeating the old refrain, "Is that all there is?" Ms. Cutler says that we are seeing the maturing of America, and are now dealing with a group that understands what she calls the "banner of the Nineties," "I can't do it alone." Time is now the most scarce resource in most families, and this factor will have to be considered by those providing both products and services.

The market can be tapped to tell marketing what to do, marketing can tell operations what to produce, and strategies can be planned to tap that market and expand the need for your services or products. At every step the staff

- must have input into the process
- must have a part in identifying and meeting the new challenge
- must be part of the solution.

At no time can you forget that your staff IS the company in the minds of your clients or customers. Keep in mind the real meaning of those two lines in the dollar sign—

—one stands for generated revenue and the other for incurred expenses, and it isn't enough to have them balance. The first must be greater than the second, and can be if you make certain that your game plan is customer driven.

2

THE IMPORTANCE OF CUSTOMER SERVICE

"To survive in today's marketplace, it is essential that we go back to the old fashioned approach of knowing your business, your customer, and your competition...these are critical elements to success."

Antonio C. Luna, Sr. Vice President
Club Resorts, Inc.

Quality—the public is no longer willing to settle for anything less. Of course, cost is a key factor in the decision to purchase any product, secure any service, or pay for any idea, but we can no longer fool ourselves into believing that discounted prices or even competitive prices are enough to get and keep customers. We are in the middle of a quality revolution.

All we have to do is listen to the T.V. or radio advertisements or look in any publication to see that delivering what is ordered isn't enough—quality separates the successful from the near-misses in every industry, organization, and company.

The most obvious need for outstanding services is noted in the various service industries. Just look around you. How much time do you, your friends, and family spend in restaurants, hotels, on airlines, in hospitals, banks, schools, or dealing with various governmental agencies? They all have the problem of gaining and retaining customers, don't they? True, governmental agencies, utilities and schools may not realize that they are dependent upon a customer base, but they are. A few years ago in California, a young legislator was irritated with the manner of several individuals encountered at a county office. After having a rerun of the experience and hearing from colleagues that they, too, had experienced similar problems, he authored a bill designed to eliminate country governments in the state and provide for the assumption of all of their duties by other government agencies. The bill **almost** passed.

What is the message? Complacency can be dangerous! No organization or company can afford to ignore the person who pays the bills—who literally **runs** the company—the customer!

It is no longer sufficient for a company to have one department, and only one department, charged with the responsibility of customer service. Customer relations and customer service awareness needs to permeate the entire organization and be integral to the behavior of every employee. More simply, customer service must be everyone's job.

This means that the truth behind the term "customer-driven" business must become an ingrained behavioral base, that steps need to be taken to develop training programs that provide for

- technical skills
- knowledge bases
- interactive skills
- tracking systems
- incentive programs
- effective management technique
- hiring/training/positioning approaches that insure job matches and provide for career tracking systems.
- appropriate motivational approaches
- the development of employee self-motivation

None of this can be done by involving only the front line people or designing mission statements that are paper-based only. It requires, for most companies, a shake-up that begins with sound strategic planning, moves into a planning and implementation stage, and continues for the life of the company.

CUSTOMER SERVICE

The demand for customer satisfaction—something many of our ancestors took for granted to the point that they believed it was literally a "birth right"—is a world-wide phenomenon. Executives in all fields are seeing a potential for using it as a powerful, competitive weapon in the war for profits.

There are key factors that govern service, insure quality, and form the base for orchestrating or managing both. It will be up to the management team in each organization or company to set the stage, design a framework, and monitor consistency. As important as these factors are to the on-going productivity and success of a company or industry, they are not difficult to identify or use. Then why have they been forgotten by so many?

We believe that the strong emphasis on technology and development created a focus on the product and caused a shift away from service, but conversely that focus is shifting rapidly. Companies as diverse as SAS (the Scandinavian airline) and Nordstroms (a Seattle based department store chain) are putting it at the front of their planning and as the focus of their advertising campaigns.

The key to the success of a customer-oriented culture is the management staff, for all businesses and organizations have demonstrated that there is a ripple effect in all aspects of production and performance. The bottom is a clear reflection—a mirror in essence—of the top. When management cares about service, quality, and performance, staff does, too.

Management training and change must come first; management commitment must be visible and consistent; only then will staff see a reason and a need to put into action what may well be written into job manuals, corporate policy, or publicity. This means that the role of management may well have to shift and begin to

- set expectations
  - of quality
  - consistency
  - caring
  - serving
- provide an individualized motivational program and climate
- identify and provide necessary resources
- build teams and give them responsibility and authority
- involve staff in problem solving and implementation
- serve as facilitators who remove obstacles and reward outstanding performance.

CUSTOMER SERVICE

The U.S. Department of Commerce foresees continued—and rapid—growth in the service industries and service jobs, and service is now the key to success in the world economic marketplace. Of even more importance is the growing awareness of industry that service is not just a by-product that generates no profits, but the key to gaining the edge that leads to profit generation. When these two pieces of information are combined, we have to recognize that the entire economic system by which we have so long lived and worked needs reworking.

Obviously, we are not going to produce fewer goods, nor are we going to consume less. It does mean, however, that fewer people will be needed to do the production level while jobs and energies will be reapportioned to the services sector.

Take a look at Epson America. At one time this computer company had branches throughout the United States as well as Japan. In the mid-eighties a new awareness led them to set up regional divisions, close the branches, and service the vendors via sales, marketing, service representatives based at the three regional offices. The foundation of this company is a product—computers and computer-related products—but as the use of those products grow, the need for related services is multiplied many times. Because they are aware of this fact, the company took a giant step in 1989. They made their major focus a service focus and implemented programs that put customer service in the forefront of their planning process. This focus went far beyond the representatives in the field, it permeated every department and division of the corporation. It was well-thought out and implemented throughout the world.

IS YOUR COMPANY OR ORGANIZATION CUSTOMER-DRIVEN?

Of course! Every one of us depends upon customers, members, patients, clients—to paraphrase poet Gertrude Stein, "a customer is a customer is a customer."

According to the last census report, about 60 percent of U.S. workers are employed in industries that do not provide tangibles. Yours may well fall into one of those categories which range all the way from wholesale retail trade through finance, insurance or real estate and on into transportation, communication, education, and utilities. Support services such as accounting, domestic help, personal care, recreation, law, or construction probably account for the fastest growing areas, but all of those mentioned are support vs product.

Just as **everyone** is a customer and a salesperson, so is **everyone** in service and production. It doesn't matter if I am in a back room on Wall Street preparing financial reports or drafting letters, I am as much a part of the service industry as are my colleagues, the telemarketers at 100 Church Street, N.Y. We all produce and serve, the process just differs, but the public is the winner or loser according to the quality of our production, and their response, in turn, dictates our success and acceptance. Companies need to make **all** of their employees aware of how important each is to the success of the business.

> **"At Embassy Suites, our success is based on service to customers, but it is not sufficient that our customers leave our hotels satisfied. Our continued success depends on their being enthusiastically satisfied with their stay, and that is our objective. Such customers are our best salespersons."**
>
> **Perry Sorenson, COO**
> **Embassy Suites**

Years ago, the importance of attitude was brought home to several of us when we were called in to work with a city library system in California. The comment of the librarian, which happily is not a common one, tells the story. When asked what she saw as the biggest obstacle to the successful operation of the library, she responded, "Patrons. This would be great place to work if they wouldn't come in and mess up all the books." Until all of us—whatever the industry—realize that customers can be the prophets of modern business, we will not be as successful as we would like. In other words, our customers can alert us to needed changes, to the success of given approaches, to needs in the marketplace, and provide the base for our growth, operation, and success. A number of studies have been conducted, and although their statistics vary somewhat, basically they all agree with the report prepared for the White House Office of Consumer Affairs in the 1970's. Did you know?

- for every complaint you hear, another 26 people have had problems and 6 (some studies say 7, and others 11) have had serious concerns.

- non-complainers tend to move to other sources for the services or products; those who tell you are more likely to come back—particularly if you handle the problem skillfully.

- the average person will tell between 9 and 11 people about problems, and those who are the most people-oriented will tell far more—up to 20 other people.

- if you resolve that problem, only 5 people will hear about it.

Consider the impact of those figures. Real estate salespeople and insurance salespeople have been hearing about them for years. If you consider that the truly successful sales people in those two fields depend upon referrals, you can see why it is important for them to provide the best service possible. They know that each customer is worth far more than the commission earned on one purchase; each customer has a long term value and is potentially an on-going source of income—direct, and indirect.

What gets in the way of service?

- attitude (some people feel degraded by the very word, and yet might well be in awe of their doctor who provides a service that can make the difference—literally—between life and death)

- lack of training (penny wise, pound foolish companies often cut training first when profits grow slim)

- poor management of human resources (the manager who takes great care to keep machinery in good working order may ignore human needs)

- pressure (pressure to produce can often result in stress and a feeling that time just isn't there to consider anything more than the delivery date)

- poor communication skills.

If we all practiced the platinum rule—do unto others as they need to have you do unto them—and remembered to consider how we would feel if we were in their place, we would probably change many of the things we do in the name of "service."

HOW WOULD YOU LIKE TO DEAL WITH YOU?

England has a value-added tax, but the real "value-added" label should be on the service we all provide. Ask yourself these questions.

- Have you ever sent a client/customer/patron an article or news clipping that relates to something of interest to him/her/them?
- Do you go out of your way to help (i.e., an open house sign is available to the neighbors of one Chicago real estate firm whenever they want to give a party)?
- Do you welcome complaints from your clientele? Do you view these complaints as a learning experience for which you would have to pay good money if you hired a research team to unearth the same information?
- Do you take time to send cards at appropriate times—birthday, holiday, etc. (i.e., One

escrow office in Los Angeles, Hillhurst Escrow, sends birthday cards out to clients)?

- Do you give back to your community (i.e., a number of cities now have ADOPT A SCHOOL programs through which businesses provide time, advice, and help to improve the school systems from which they later draw their greatest resources—people)?

> **"You never stop selling—ideas, services, or products, and your communication can determine your success."**
>
> **from EVERYONE IS A CUSTOMER by Elizabeth Kearney and Michale Bandley**

It is time that we take another look at our business world and realize that customer service is, and always has been, a strategic tool and a positive force for increasing profits and reducing costs. The impact of this understanding can be multiplied many times over once we realize that as the client base grows—and potentially it does with every birth—we must be able to deliver both product and service effectively, efficiently, dependably, courteously, and this will demand planning and systemization.

SERVICE IS BIG BUSINESS

Service is big business, and it is characterized by a changing attitude in the last 20th century. No longer is it degrading to serve others. It is a fact of life that the service umbrella has grown and now extends over many diverse and integral parts of our marketplace.

UNSKILLED LABOR OR ENTRY LEVEL POSITIONS

It is no longer accurate to assume that many of the unskilled jobs will be providing a means for new entrants into our society to become acclimated to it. Instead, corporations have set up systems that are often highly automated and require skills that preclude the hiring of unskilled individuals. The result—a need for more extensive training and a need for industry to develop the training process to insure that the outcomes match the needs. Educational institutions are often slow to change and in many parts of the country have not yet accommodated for employment demands.

In the early 1920's there were a number of so-called "colleges" that trained domestic help; in the 1940's, 1950's, and 1960's, we went through a period where it was almost impossible to even find domestic labor. Companies stepped in, devised systems which streamlined the process, and provided fast, efficient service, guaranteed to satisfy the client. A national franchise like Merry Maids is an excellent example of such companies—they saw a service need and devised a means to fill it.

According to a recent *Wall Street Journal* article, a nanny's college is beginning, and those working mothers who were unable to find good child care will be able to tap into a trained cadre of nannys. Again, someone saw a need, designed a system, and marketed it.

Service is multi-faceted:

- the industrial world stresses production, but as competition increases, more and more service support personnel are needed.

- professions have become increasingly aware of the need for greater flexibility and a willingness to change. Accounting is a changing field, but not one bit more so than teaching. Medicine and law are also facing changes (franchises have sprung up and HMO services are increasing medical competition). There is also an increased demand for greater and more extensive service availability while there continues to be an emphasis upon quality accountability and cost effectiveness.

- in the last few years technology has driven many of our business changes, and now that technological revolution has moved into a customer revolt. What has been created must be serviced and the on-going success of any company will depend upon the quality of that service and the credibility of those providing it.

Whatever the industry or company, the basis of service is the fact that the provider must keep the buyer happy if the buyer is to continue to want the service or product. We only have to look around to see that the trend is to move to a more personalized level of customer interaction.

- Large restaurants are giving way to small, intimate cafes.

- Large department stores are finding themselves in competition with numerous boutiques which are able to attract many of their once-loyal customers, so the large stores are putting in boutique-like divisions which can provide similar services at better prices.

- Bankers are also aware of the need for more

personalized customer services, and many banks are now sending notices to their customers and inviting them to make use of their personal banking services. In fact, a number of banks—even major banks—have set up staffs who are assigned to the clients to insure a more personalized service.

This increased interest in personalized banking service is also reflected in the advertisements which stress the importance of the customer and promise "old-fashioned" service.

There is a great deal of speculation about the reasons for the shift in focus. Some feel the increased security and comfort levels of the population have given them the luxury that once belonged only the rich—the luxury of demanding the best in product, quality, and service. It is not important to know why the revolution in attitude took place. What is important is that it did! Now, it is up to businesses to adapt, survive and succeed.

3

A NEW WAY TO LOOK AT CUSTOMER RELATIONS

"Customer service isn't a department or a 'theme for the day—it's a mission, the reason your business exists."

Susan Huber, Vice President
Daseke Management Company of America, Inc.

Customers are a company's only true external asset and employees, the major internal asset. Without the former, there is no need for the latter. It really doesn't matter what your capital outlay, how prestigious your offices, how detailed your procedures—customers won't talk about any of those things. They don't care how you finance your undertakings or integrate your systems. All they talk about is how well your staff served them, related to them, or cared about them.

According to the CEO of Scandinavian Airlines, Jan Carlzon, last year each of their "10 million customers came in contact with approximately five SAS employees, and this contact lasted an average of 15 seconds each time. Thus, SAS is created 50 million times a year, 15 seconds at a time. These 50 million moments of truth are the moments that ultimately determine whether SAS will succeed or fail as a company. They are the moments when we must prove to our customers that SAS is their best alternative."

Consider this

- How many customers do you have?

- How many of your employees do these individuals encounter and for how long each time?

- Now, calculate the moments of truth in your company.

If you are really interested in creating a customer-driven company, then there must be decentralization of responsibility and authority. The "15 second" people must be involved in the process. Rule books work only up to a point. There are situations where the rules won't work or have never been written to cover them. In such instances, you need to have trained your frontline so well that they can think, act, and make decisions that are appropriate, both

- Internally—the company is protected, made to

look good, and procedures are followed to the extent possible, and

- Externally—the customer is made to feel that you care and value him/her, that you put him/her first, and that the company literally runs for the customers.

When you take this step, you risk upsetting tradition. The most inflexible pyramid in the world lies not in the so-called pyramid scheme, but rather in the corporate organizational pattern.

This structure is no longer practical in service-driven businesses. Companies need to reorganize and create a more horizontal structure. In such a structure, it is up to top management to become a true leader, to create an environment that nurtures individuals and maximizes their talents for the welfare of the customer, and thus the company. This leader can no longer be the penthouse prophet—isolated and autocratic. Instead, circumstances dictate a far more diverse and varied role. This person must be a

- futurist
- strategist
- motivator
- coach
- teacher
- team player

Mid-management will have to assume greater responsibility for analyzing problems, securing and managing resources, and coaching and supporting staff—those who are literally on the front lines daily. Once management opts for a customer-driven plan, their job becomes that of a facilitator and monitor, serving those who serve the customer.

> **"Management sets the tone; staff implements it."**
>
> **from EVERYONE IS A CUSTOMER by E. Kearney and M. Bandley**

The front line employee also needs to assume new responsibilities. It is this group that must be ready, and able, to respond to the needs and problems of the customers. And, a new understanding of the word customer is needed. Everyone with whom we interact is a customer, for we are trying to "sell" an idea, a concept, a service, or a product in every encounter.

By reshuffling responsibility patterns in this way, companies can insure a more positive image because those with whom they interact have the empowerment to respond to each individual's unique needs in a timely and courteous way.

WHAT HAS TO CHANGE?

The roles played out by every member of the company must change in order to make this system work. The traditional corporate executive assumes a directive role, issues orders or instructions, and watches decisions flow from the top down. The new "breed" alters this role and keeps the big picture in mind, understands the competition and shops it, and sets the tone for the entire operation.

HOW CAN CHANGE BE TRIGGERED?

Listen! To the customers, to the staff, and to what you hear about your competitors.

First, realize that the jargon that you and your staff depend upon as a form of communication shorthand may well lose the customer. We may not recognize a Q fare, but few of us have trouble understanding **Supersaver** fares. Find out what your own particular market prizes, and show how you can meet those needs or wants. For example, if you ran an airline, you would be aware of the fact that

- student travelers want "cheap fares"
- business travelers are time conscious
- executives are time and comfort conscious
- government travelers are money conscious
- family travelers are bargain conscious.

Using this data, you could build your campaigns, but it is not enough to tell about your service or bargains unless you also realize that once offered, people resent it when standard "perks" are withdrawn. Many business travelers shifted from their "favorite airline" in 1989 when several carriers indicated that the "mileage bonuses" would be severely restructured. Recognizing this, several other carriers sent personalized letters to frequent travelers noting that they were not altering their bonus structures. As frequent travelers ourselves, we weren't surprised to find that many of our colleagues were shifting allegiance because of the changes—and threatened changes. The interesting part of this scenario is that many of us who travel 10 and 12 days per month never get around to using that mileage anyway. **But we don't want it taken away!** Perhaps we need to consider putting some psychologists in the strategy planning loop.

There is a real need to understand motivators in order to do the needed strategy planning. For example, many years ago, a major prepared food vendor came out with a mix that needed only water to produce a truly outstanding cake. The package was well thought out and very attractive, the product was excellent, but it sat for months on store shelves. Few takers. After considering the psychological element involved, a new approach was tried—the egg was taken out of the mix, the directions altered to tell the cook to put in an egg, and the advertising began to stress how good the cook would feel about the cake "created." What happened? You guessed it! That product became an overnight hit and is still being marketed successfully. Why? The original mix was too easy to prepare. Customers felt left out and didn't get any personal satisfaction because they really weren't involved in the process.

A little imagination can make a major difference in attracting and keeping customers. For example, a number of airlines have used the "buy a ticket-get a second one free" approach to stimulate travel during the slower months, and others have tied mileage to the use of long distance travel and hotel stays. By ploys such as these, they work within the process long known to be successful—people want "something" for nothing.

Your front line people are closest to the customer base. They hear more complaints, know when something is working, and may well have some excellent ideas about ways to improve service and product. Listen, support, and reward your front line.

In order to know how this works, just think of all the times you and your friends have said "if only." "If only there were a vending machine in the hall." "If only there were a way to use the phone system more effectively." Each "if only"—the staff's or a customer's—has the potential of improving both service and profit.

When people understand where you are going, recognize their role in the corporate plan and identify with the company goals, many of them will be willing to go the "extra mile" to make it work. This means that communication is vital to your success. Consider how many times employees are called upon to make another person's dream a reality. Think how much faster it might happen if the employee knew that he/she had part of the dream—i.e., profit sharing and stock options.

Check your company to see if an internal attitude adjustment is needed. Don't fear your competition—**use it!** It seems hard to understand why competition in the locker room is a spur to success whereas it has far less impact in the board room. We may fear the loss of a market, but all too often we don't take the steps that could prevent it.

- Have you checked out your competition?
    - bought the product?
    - traveled with them (transportation industry)?
    - studied their annual reports?
    - followed their ad campaigns?
- Have you checked out your own operation?
    - brought in mystery shoppers? These are professionals who evaluate your company and its services from a customer's point of view.
    - set up a complaint system and a process for monitoring complaints?

  - involved your front line in planning?

  - provided training on a consistent, on-going basis?

  - encouraged creative thinking?

  - fostered the talents of your employees?

  - done an item by item analysis of what works, and what doesn't work?

- Have you taken time to do some market studies?

  - using your own staff as experts on market responses?

  - prepared and used questionnaires to gain information?

  - studied prepared data from various sources?

  - made this a team effort?

After you have done all of that, you may decide that certain facets of the company need to undergo change. You many find that you need to take some 90 degree turns. For example, do you have to be 100% better in one given area or could you accomplish the same goal by being 1% better in 100 areas? What we are trying to say is—change your thinking process, get off the old track, and realize that you can't get to a new goal on an old road.

For instance, stop considering your outlay and expenses as negatives—try seeing them as opportunities for improving your overall competitiveness. See your staff as your greatest asset and invest in them—invest trust, responsibility, and training. It pays dividends back.

This doesn't mean that all expenses are positives. Instead take a long look and see what is no longer contributing directly to your goals. For example, if you run an airline, then the yardstick would be

> Is this expenditure contributing to the goal of serving those travelers? If it is, keep it. If it isn't, cut it.

Let us again use SAS as an example and quote from their CEO.

> "Once we had identified the clear goal of serving business travelers, the cuts were easy to identify and we knew they wouldn't hurt us. For example, business travelers were not interested in helping us pay to maintain a department that promoted tourist trips...SAS had a

> 40 person market survey department that churned out extensive market analyses...a vital function as long as all the decisions were made by a few executives isolated from the customers. But once we passed responsibility out to the front line we no longer needed so many market surveyors—our decisions were being made by people who had direct contact with the market all the time."

This same analysis base can be used to streamline paperwork. Often paper flow grows beyond all logic because no one wants to be left out or miss anyone. Take a look at your manuals, instructions, policies, and files. What is being duplicated? What is really necessary? Evaluate and toss—keep only those that are **really necessary!**

The most significant internal change is a change in employee attitude. All too often, staff, management, and administration make service secondary in the scheme of operation. In fact, often it was seen as the responsibility of the "customer service" department. When you make it the responsibility and driving force in the **entire** organization, you have introduced a strategy that cannot help but have major implications and impact. The front line employees are now the key to the company's success, and their feeling of self-worth is enhanced by this new focus and by the training that must, of necessity, be provided to make the focus work. They find themselves in the limelight, and the Hawthorne Effect—added attention and greater expectations trigger greater success and dedication—occurs.

Of course, the new focus demands a new communication system. **Everyone** needs to know about and understand the corporate mission and game plan. Without information, they can't assume responsibility, but with it they can't avoid it. How will you know it works? Simple, when the top executive can leave and all operations continue smoothly then delegation has been effective and responsibility has been assumed. When this happens, you will know that the traditional system is no longer in operation. In that system the executive was a decision maker for whom others supplied data which he or she processed and then reacted to by establishing direction or issuing orders. He was the only one who saw the "big picture," so he, or the executive team, made all of the really important decisions—no one else had the information base to do so.

There are inherent problems in this traditional system. It is impossible for any one person to investigate every issue, become an expert in every aspect of the operation, or truly understand all facets of the on-going process—so many decisions simply never get made. The staff never has the "big picture," the executive can't do everything, and together their efforts become counter productive. There is no doubt that companies run under this format take a heavy toll on their leaders who are "anchored" to their work.

> **"A good leader inspires other men with confidence in him; a great leader inspires men with confidence in themselves."**
>
> **Anonymous**

Real leadership demands delegation, and when it is used, the executive must begin with a goal, devise a strategy, communicate it, delegate authority and responsibility, create a secure environment that promotes their use, and develop evaluation measures that prompt movement in the right direction. The easiest management technique is "do it or decide it yourself." The hardest is "let the one on the front line who has the real knowledge of day-to-day operations and related problems make decisions related to that operation."

THE VIEW FROM CLOUD NINE

The best way to develop the kind of leadership needed is to get out of your rut, move up to cloud nine, and look down on the layout below. Strategies are best when the "big picture" is viewed, and needs and resources are assessed and managed with it in mind.

The successful business leader in today's service-driven company needs to manage four things: finances, production, technology, and human resources, and follow the success chain.

The Success Chain

Set goals

•
•

Communicate them clearly.

•
•

Train others to implement the goals.

•
•

Encourage others to assume responsibility for the goals.

•
•

Provide the support and security needed by staff.

•
•

Foster flexibility, creativity, and innovation.

•
•

Reward success.

With all of this in place, we will find that leadership will be redefined. The best leaders will be those who

- listen
- communicate
- educate
- foster talent
- demand loyalty
- delegate
- and create the right environment for success!

4

THE CUSTOMER'S POINT OF VIEW

"Never take a customer for granted."

W.E. Deal
Regional Sales Manager
Prof. Photography Division
Kodak

'We are the most important person in your business!" That's every customer's view, and it is imperative that you believe us! We are your business, we provide the base of your income, the market for your products, and the PR you need.

A 1976 study by the National Council of Physical Distributors noted that customers would reduce their purchases by 22.4 percent if customer services standards fell by only 5%. Turn that around. What might happen if you increased that service by just 5% and filled the voids that competitors have left?

How can you do that? Mount your own market study—not an expensive, long-range study—via a well-planned questionnaire that could be done by your staff or mystery shoppers. Ask some specific questions about your product or service, and then ask four vital question—the keys to filling that void.

- Have you ever used this service (or bought a similar product) before?
- What did you like best about it?
- What suggestions could you make to improve it?
- What would you like to see offered that isn't?

Have 100 randomly selected people answer this questionnaire. If 10 have the same answers (content, not words), you have some meaningful information. What did they like best? Least? What do they want? Now use this information. Make certain that you are offering what they like. Make certain that your promotions note how you differ from those things that they like least, and begin planning your next offering around what they don't have but want. **Simple, effective**, and **profitable.**

Clients and customers fall into two major categories—those who are results oriented and those who are process oriented. The first group will tell you when they are upset, they will point out the problem, they will share their views for change, but the second group is less likely to let you in on their dissatisfaction—they just move on.

They are like the person described in the following poem:

Never Look Back

Mother taught me very well
To keep my poise and never yell.
And that is what I always do
Despite my problems, complaints are few.

My silver's dirty, the orders wrong,
But my smile's in place though my sigh is long.
That man came in after me
And got his food immediately.

I try my best to catch the eye
Of the waiter who is passing by,
But he is really very skilled,
In avoidance he was probably drilled.

I leave the table and go to find
A suit—or two—I wouldn't mind,
But I really want to look around
For colors, styles, and costs abound.

THE CUSTOMER'S POINT OF VIEW

A snooty clerk disdains to tell
Me if my choices are going well.
She seems annoyed that I can't see
Just what I want that pleases me.

She's curt and rude and bored I see,
But I'm as polite as I can be.
For mother said it would never do
When one is rude, don't make it two.

I left the store in mild dismay,
And headed home, but on the way
I stopped nearby to use full serve
But the attendant thought I had my nerve.

Did I complain to anyone?
No, that's not the way my life is run.
Ladies and gentlemen don't make a scene
On such behavior they're not keen.

Instead, they just turn away.
You lost a customer today.

Since some 70% of the population is process oriented, you can't afford to ignore their tendency to avoid waves and problems. You need to know what they think! If they walk away rather than initiating negatives, how can you learn what irritated them or if your product or service is meeting the needs of your clients or customers?

First: Identify your market and target it. You can't sell or serve the three markets (high-end, mid-range, or low-end) the same way. The needs are different, the reactions are different, and your approach needs to match.

> Motel Six ends its radio commercials with the line "We'll leave the light on for you," while Leona Helmsley stresses the concept that the "queen takes care of every detail for her guests." One well-known restaurant chain stresses its family atmosphere and competitive pricing while another stresses ambiance and the quiet elegance that provides the unobtrusive service needed while mergers are discussed.
>
> Companies that try to meet all markets risk losing their market share in all of them.

Second: Consider what makes your clientele comfortable and then provide it. Part of the customers' security comes from subliminal messages.

> Real estate agents know that they are often judged by the car that they drive. A large, elegant car denotes success, success comes from selling houses, houses sold in large numbers mean that the person does a good job and meets the needs of the client, hence, he or she must be able to meet "my needs."

Doctors know that the waiting room needs to give the patient a message—this doctor is concerned about my health. So the doctor may want to put some health-related magazines around the waiting room to reinforce the image of concern.

At the same time, patients want to know that the doctor is not overcharging, so the furnishings need to be attractive but not too upscale or expensive. It is important to deal with experts, so the office probably needs to display diplomas and honors.

Whatever your industry or field, take time to build rapport and mirror your client/customer. We are most comfortable with those who are most like us, so make "me feel comfortable when I am with you."

You can build a stronger communication bridge if you will mirror my listening language. After all, we are all more comfortable with others like us, so

> If I am a visual person who speaks rapidly, tell me what you want me to know in visual terms—make me see it—and do so quickly.

> If I am an auditory person who enunciates carefully, make certain that your message is given in words I will understand ("Listen, tell,

hear, sound") and is spoken with precision—verbally and audibly.

If I am a kinesthetic (feeling) person, slow down and help me "understand, grasp" the meaning of your message.

Third: Plan your subliminal approach with your customers' reaction in mind.

- Beautiful packages should be easy to open (cost is important, but the customer's reaction is more important).

- Advertising should give only one message at a time—never mix product and service messages.

- Will your clientele react best to traditional, conservative stationary? the high tech look? color? the muted look? It may be your first and last chance to make an impression, make certain that that impression is the one you want.

- Is the dress of your staff creating the right image? The three-piece suit may make some clients uncomfortable, while the hard hat will hardly do in the board room.

- What is the telephone quotient of your staff? Do they smile, answer promptly, take messages graciously, avoid the hold button, show interest, follow-through, return calls?

- How do your letters come across? Good information alone is not enough—if typing is sloppy, or the layout unattractive, it is like presenting a gourmet dinner on a dirty plate.

- What are your guidelines for response time, turn-around time, product knowledge, complaint resolutions?

Consistency is an essential element in success, and that means that **all** of the above elements must be in place and working well. When one area breaks down it negates the value of the others in the customer's mind. One of the best examples of this occurred just recently.

The brilliant California sun and the splashing waves along the beach in Malibu, California, had put a stern CEO into a mellow mood when he was jolted by the impact of metal meeting metal. His small sports car was thrown toward the shoulder as a semi rolled on down Pacific Coast Highway. The car still ran, he gunned it, followed the truck for several miles, caught up to it at a stop light and yelled at the driver to pull over. The driver gestured insultingly and drove on. Furious, the CEO turned to return to his office, but he had noted the name on the truck. When he got back in to the plant, he called his Chief Operating Officer and told him to cancel the contract negotiations with XYZ trucking company.

The message traveled fast, 1 1/2 hours later, the owner of the trucking company was on the phone asking why. The response was pointed and brief—"I can't afford to trust my loads to any company whose drivers are careless and unconcerned."

> **"Quality Customer Relations is customer satisfaction. It is an attitude, a pursuit—accomplished by working together, aspiring to the fullness of our potential, always in pursuit of higher standards."**
>
> **Sue Kraemer, Tele-Sales Manager**
> **Eric Herman**
> **Steve Moyer**
> **Hallmark Cards**

The message—your total service package must reflect the values of those whom you serve. That means people, equipment, product, and interaction.

Because this is so vital, many companies are now hiring mystery shoppers or putting quality control experts into the field. Later chapters will deal with both approaches, but there are some questions you can ask that will give you valuable guidelines.

- If we walked into your office, what would we see first? Is the front desk manned by a well-dressed person, attractively "packaged"? Is that person likely to be chatting on the phone and unaware that we came in? Is the desk neat? Is there food on it? Is that person chewing gum? **Have you even looked lately?**

- Are the company vehicles, or those personal ones used for business, clean, well-maintained, freshly painted? **The vehicles are a visual representation of your company and reflect your attitude.**

- Can we even find your office once we find the address? Are there signs, are they clear, are office numbers easily visible? **It is a rare customer who gets excited about hunting for an office.**

- What about your office? Would you be willing to have "guests" join you there? Even if it is filled with projects, is there order? Are waste baskets empty or overflowing? Are the windows clean? Are ashtrays empty? Is it attractive? **It tells a great deal about you and how you will handle our business!**

- Is that consistency carried over into the quality of the product. **Loyal customers only stay loyal as long as the product or service provides consistent quality and performance.**

- What is the mood in your office? Are there harmonious relations? If not, tensions impact negatively even on those "outside" of them. Have you taken the time and made an effort to train your staff to function as a team? Do they understand—truly understand—each other and why one person may tend to take charge while another stresses the importance of details? **If they don't, clashes may well occur, and clashes pulsate negatively.**

- What is the office environment like? Is layout conducive to productivity? Fatigue? Is the lighting soft and calming? Are support services and support equipment readily available or at great distances? **Is time wasted and fatigue created because of poor planning?**

- Are staff members treated as valuable resources? Given responsibility? Given credit and incen-

Building Rapport

We spoke earlier about mirroring, and when this is coupled with "key" words, the impact is truly impressive. In order to know which words anchor the communication bridge, it is necessary to learn to recognize the types of people we encounter. There are six basic behavioral styles (**Leaders, Persuaders, Patient People, Careful People, Reserved People** and **Independents**), which combine into 19 composites. When we learn to "read" them and ourselves, we can then understand them and respond more appropriately to meet their needs or adjust our behaviors so they are less jarring. Before we tell you how to do this, we must first give you some warnings.

- Most of us change to some degree every six to eighteen months, so you can't get a permanent "reading."

- We all have an image we project to the world, one that appears when we are under stress, pressure, or when relaxed, and these two combine and are viewed as our public image.

- We may have as many as two or three public images and we could have another two or three latent ones. You need to read the person "in front of you now" not yesterday or last year.

- We may have as many as two or three public images and we could have another two or three latent ones. You need to read the person "in front of you now" not yesterday or last year.

- The clues that let you "read" people should be considered together, for no one clue will give the whole picture.

Now let's walk you through a quick training session in how to identify each of the primary styles.

The first style is that of the **Leaders.**

Pace: They walk fast, talk fast, and have only two speeds—fast and faster.

Dress: They tend to wear corporate dress (For men that means a dark suit, white shirts, tie with some red in it, dark shoes—probably wing-tip, and dark socks. For women that means colors such as navy blue, black, wine or maroon, taupe, grey, or winter white; minimal make-up; classically simple jewelry; natural-hued hose; short or pulled up hairdos; and pumps).

Job: They tend to assume positions that give authority; if not they may assume some anyway. They want a challenge, to know the big picture, chance to problem solve and work on challenges.

Manner: They are direct, straight forward, directive, and assertive.

Desk: They hate to waste time, so their desk is covered with organized stacks. It takes too much time to clear the desk off and too much time to find things if it gets messy—hence each stack has a purpose.

Key Words: They respond best to words that fit their motivational needs, such as: results, profit, productivity, action, big picture, challenge and authority.

The second style to consider is that of the **Persuaders**.

Pace: They also have only two speeds—fast and faster.

Dress: They tend to dress very fashionably, as fashionably as their job permits.

Job: They are happiest when they can interact with enthusiastic, energetic people, so tend to hold positions that permit that—sales being a good example.

Manner: They never encounter strangers, those are just people they haven't met yet. They are warm, friendly, and outgoing.

Desk: They seldom take time to clean up their desk which is rather like the "black hole"—things disappear. True, they reappear later.

Key Words: They respond best when ideas are introduced, such as results, profit, recognition, caring, excitement, enthusiasm, quick, support.

Independent People are the third results-oriented style.

Pace: They tend to prefer a fast pace as well.

Dress: They wear what they darn well please although if it pleases them to look corporate, they will.

Job: They are often individuals who enjoy owning their own company, or prefer to work for someone who will tell them what is wanted, set the parameters, and then get out of their way and let them do it. They need to run their own show.

Manner: They are often direct, sometimes overly so, always straight forward, and occasionally blunt.

Desk: Don't understand how the rest of the world is able to fit everything onto one desk. Their work spreads out over their desk, other pieces of furniture, even chairs and the floor at times.

Key Words: They respond to many of the same key words that leaders are motivated by plus "innovative, control, and problem solving."

Patient People tend to get along with everyone, and although their style is process-oriented, they are such team players that even results-oriented people work very well with them.

Pace: They prefer to move at a slower pace and have time to weigh the pros and cons before taking action.

Dress: They are people who wear classic attire which never seems to go out of style or wear out.

Job: They tend to enter fields that require specialization, and they are willing to take the time needed to prepare for the role.

Manner: They have a diplomatic manner which conceals their own frustrations and dismay from others.

Desk: They tend to have a neat, but not compulsively neat, desk.

Key Words: They respond best to information which is presented to them in the following key words: stable, secure, traditional, analytical, thorough, teamwork, and harmonious. They need to know that projects and undertakings will produce these outcomes or have these characteristics.

Careful People deal well with details and seem to be the watchdogs of our systems. They, too, are process-oriented.

Pace: They adjust their pace to fit the situation although they prefer not to be rushed.

Dress: They usually wear clothing that is matched and blended.

Job: They tend to take jobs that require precision work, detailed approached, and a high level of accuracy. Many times the job requires that they be proficient in the use of equipment or machines.

Manner: They strive to be tactful, but that doesn't mean they may not think something else. Also, they seldom forget, and those who work with them need to remember that they don't forget!

Desk: They reveal their organizational skills and need for structure by having a place for everything and everything in its place on their desk and in their physical world (check out those closets sometime).

Key Words: They are motivated by many of the words that motivate **Patient People** plus detailed, precise, technical, accurate or perfectionism.

Reserved People are the final process-oriented style.

Pace: They also adjust pace to fit the needs of the situation.

Dress: They dress like either the Careful or the Patient People, but differ in one respect. The Reserved People get dressed in the morning and then forget about it for the rest of the day. That means that there are times when ties go askew, hose get runs, smudges appear and are never noticed.

Job: They enjoy working with ideas and concepts and may choose a career that permits them to work alone on such assignments.

Manner: They are often considered aloof, reserved, or distant. None of these terms is really accurate, for these people are warm and very friendly toward those who have been admitted to the "inner circle." But the rest of us should honor their need for privacy and give them the respect they need.

Desk: They hate clutter and keep it off the desk or out of the surroundings if at all possible.

Key Words: They respond best when ideas are presented logically, sequentially, and in a well-organized way. They need to hear the words that indicate that, too.

If you will use the above clues to "read" your clients and then use the key words to convey your points, you will find that the communication bridge is built more rapidly and that travel across it is far easier and more rewarding.

By mirroring the customer's manner and style and using the key words, you can establish the rapport that is so vital to interaction. In addition, you will be able to defuse most tense situations. Since anger is a three stage process:

This "vicious circle" leading to anger can generally be defused easily at the first two stages by solving the problem, showing the other person you are striving to solve the problem, and supplying the information in the right key words. For example, the results-oriented styles are not interested in how you plan to do it, just do it, whereas the process-oriented individuals will want to have the details.

By doing this you will be able to turn a potentially negative situation into a positive one. When you are concerned about the customers needs, let them know in their own words and via their own style. They will feel more comfortable and be assured that all will be well. Your concern and action—expressed as they will best understand it—are the keys to keeping them and their good will.

5

ARE YOUR EMPLOYEES AN ASSET OR A LIABILITY?

"Managing (companies) is a lot like flying a kite. Make sure the wind is right (marketing), the kite is in good condition (quality), and let everyone feel your gentle tug (direction and training)...."

William Verwolf
General Manager
Union Camp Corporation

"Who's that? John Wayne—can't be, he's dead!" But the voice was certainly John Wayne's, and he was telling us what to look at 37,000 feet below. The tedium of the flight was certainly broken as we listened in fascination to this "hero" telling us more about our flight on American Airlines. Later, we were delighted to hear "Gregory Peck" talk to us about the movie we were going to see, and still later another hero was heard over the loud speaker. All of these voices were the Captain's whose talents were making a long flight far more fun for all of us. We have continued to travel on this airline as often as possible because the extra touches show a concern and interest in us as customers. This captain was an asset to the company, and the value of such an asset can't be measured in dollars or time on the job.

As someone once said, the most important part of service involves personal contact. The person on the front line makes an immediate impact on the customer or client, but he/she can't do it alone. Every sale, every service, every idea has to be backed up efficiently and effectively by the "hidden employees." "Hidden" only in the sense that the customer never sees them; never in the sense that what they do does not have a direct impact upon success.

Since your greatest company asset is its employee base, then you need to evaluate it just as you would evaluate all other facets of your organization. Make certain that you hire only the best, maintain them well (train, recognize and reward), and supervise appropriately so that a true team spirit is built and maintained.

You can change behavior, but you can't change values, and behaviors reflect the values one holds. That is why some people seem to know just what to do and others always do just the opposite. Often, people seem to be unable to see a cause and effect relationship between their words or actions and your responses. Why? In some instances this void is a direct reflection of inner qualities, values and attitudes, but in others it is a lack of awareness training. The latter you can work with, the former is beyond your control.

One of the greatest costs of doing business is staffing. When we hear about a company or organization that is in financial trouble, they don't rush out to cut spending on liquid paper or envelopes—they reduce staff. The cost is staggering from the very first day.

Once you decide to staff, you must advertise, interview, evaluate, and then train. If you are dealing with upper levels of staffing, you will have related expenses ranging from the "head hunter's fee" to moving expenses for the new hire. If you don't do it well the first time, there will be turnover—there will be turnover anyway, just because of normal living patterns and shifts—and that turnover can slow down operations, and reduce general efficiency. In addition to the direct costs involved in the hiring process, there are the numerous hidden costs—orientation, supervision, and the time they take to "fit" into the new job.

Of course, mistakes add heavily to that cost—severance pay, distress suits, workman's compensation in some cases, and unemployment insurance. It is very hard to get rid of a poor employee, and next to impossible to find a great one according to personnel consultants. This is particularly true since our entire employment process is designed to leave out the most important elements—behaviors.

The hiring process usually follows a certain pattern:

- note a vacancy or upcoming vacancy
- develop a job description
- design a flyer
- contact an agency or consultant or run advertisements
- set up interviews and request applications
- review the application to determine the applicant's:
    - experience
    - educational background
    - noted skills levels
    - quality of recommendations
    - organizational skills as shown on resume and application
- check out recommendations
- administer tests, if appropriate
- set up interviews to make personal evaluations of the applicant's:
    - appearance
    - manner
    - communication skills

- overall impact

Much time and effort—it all costs money—goes into this process. It should do the job, but we seldom fire individuals because they lack skills needed to perform the job—we found that out in the selection process and didn't hire. **Why do we fire** or **why are we dissatisfied**? Generally because the employee:

- takes too much authority
- doesn't take on enough responsibility
- can't get along with other employees
- is too friendly and uses business time for personal interaction
- works too slowly
- is disorganized
- has poor follow-through
- ignores details
- is a perfectionist

Every one of these items is behaviorally based, but very few of the screening techniques are designed to identify needed job behaviors. We leave out one of the most important factors—the one that in the long run can eat up our profit base. Yet, with tools like **JOB CHECK**, which we use with our clients, it is possible to pre-determine the behaviors needed and then look for those behaviors in applicants and train those already in position to achieve a closer match.

When the job is properly identified with a tool such as JOB CHECK and the needed behaviors and the specific tasks are known, it is possible to determine the kind of person needed and then draft the initial job descriptions and advertisement to ensure that they attract those who fit best. Thus, the first "cut" is made by applicants themselves.

Of course, it is easier to hire when you only consider technical skills, background/education, and experience. You may go on to consider the applicant's ability to use the tools or equipment involved, the extent to which the job technology has been mastered, and even the person's personal resources e.g., someone in public relations). But this method, although cost effective in the short run, often falls short of providing you with the person best suited to the position.

So what do you do?

There are some **Do's** and **Don'ts** that need to be considered as you take control of your hiring process.

- **Do** make sure that your employees reflect the diverse ethnic and religions backgrounds, including gender, of your customers and clients. **You must, that's the law!**

- **Don't** violate the equal employment opportunity laws. You must be careful about the information you seek and the manner in which you seek it.

    - As long as that information is used to determine the probable performance level on the job, your processing and interview will remain within the law.

- **Do** be sure that all questions asked are job-related. There are questions that cannot be asked, and they may vary from state to state, but some cross state boundaries—race, religion, age, and politics.

Remember, people don't take jobs thinking, "Great, now here is another chance to fail." They are generally excited about the opportunity and want to do the best job possible. All too often, we don't give them the information they need to succeed. We don't define the behavioral requirements of the position because we don't know them, at least not consciously.

ONCE ON THE JOB

People tend to define jobs by what is produced, and we tend to determine our own self-worth by the jobs we hold. Ask someone for a self-description and they rarely tell you about their hobbies, families, interests. They say, "I'm a teacher, doctor, plumber, writer, etc." The American work ethic is such that our job and our self-worth are often closely intertwined. It is important for employers to understand this and provide ways to insure that employees are effective and satisfied with their jobs.

You need to stress:

- the behaviors that will be needed in the job
- the results you want to see
- the results your customers or clients want to see—in terms of behaviors, such as
  - friendly service
  - quick response to questions or problems
  - knowledge of the product or service
  - a willingness to make decisions and take action
  - and someone who makes a good first impression.

> **"I realize that people never buy logically, they buy emotionally and they base their decision on 'Do I or don't I like the salesperson?'"**
>
> **Susan Bixler, President**
> **Professional Image, Inc.**

You also need to consider your clientele and then match your front line people to them. We recently spoke to a professor at Long Beach State University in California. She was very unhappy in her new position. Although she was well-known in her field, had achieved a reputation as an authority in her field, and was respected by those in industry, she was having a terrible time "reaching" her students. She had forgotten one thing, graduate students and college seniors have a subliminally negative reaction to being told what to do by someone who does not inspire confidence. It was unimportant to them that she had those credentials They had never heard of her, but they did see her every day, and her dress and demeanor was that of a peer—not a professor. She sincerely wanted to teach them the foundations of her field, but without a change to a professional mode of speech, dress and manner, her efforts were doomed to failure.

Consider staffing a world class resort. The clientele

might enjoy working with a tennis pro who was young, skilled, and tanned, but the General Manager who answered to that description would hardly inspire respect.

Start with the customers and build their needs into the job description and behavioral needs.

Does that mean that you need be concerned only with those jobs that involve direct customer contact? Yes! But, don't draw the definition of customer too tightly—everyone in your company is a customer. They must work and interact with each other, and motivate themselves and each other.

How does that impact upon the hiring process? Greatly!

Never hire internal competitors. Hire a team player.

Build your team. No one can do everything, but there is a tendency for us to like our own style and way of doing things so well that we will look around for someone just like us—it's comfortable. When you do that, you do not balance the team—you double its strengths while doubling its weaknesses, too.

**Never hire your clones;
hire your complements.**

We know that values clashes often destroy marriages, but what we often fail to consider is that those same values can clash at work with equally disastrous results.
Remember:

- Workaholics and clock watchers seldom make a "good marriage."
- Negativism and positivism are poles apart and can destroy working relations and harmony.
- The Rebel and the Conservative seldom agree.
- The Coach and the Dictator take different roads.
- The Manipulator and the Team Player are eternally at odds.

The real issues basic to job success go beyond technical knowledge, education, or experience. A person may be very successful in one company, attempt the same level and kind of work in another company and fail. Why? The interpersonal demands and values are different.

Identify the behavioral styles needed and share this information with the employees.

YOU AND YOUR VALUES

It is only fair to share your personal values and expectations with your employees. We tend to believe that we need to surround ourselves with others who feel as we do and are motivated as we are. Because of this, we also judge others by our own motivators and values.

The person who begins checking the clock at 4:55 p.m. and edges into the office a little later every day, will find us becoming increasingly disenchanted with them as staff members. We want employees who make a commitment to:

- quality work
- our goals
- our customers and clients.

We want to know that the person will stay late if an emergency arises, and will go "the extra mile." What we have learned is that the extra mile is never crowded—unfortunately—but those that are on it are those with initiative and creativity.

We use **VALUES CHECK** to help us and our clients select those employees whose values mesh with ours and our company's. There are only six to consider, but they provide essential information related to the job match. Just remember that **Values —"R BASIC."**

RBASIC

R stands for **Research** and information. Some of us want every detail, but there are those who want no details, just the "big picture."

B stands for **Beauty**. There are those who will only work where there is beauty. Others work any where as long as the equipment needed is there.

A stands for **Affluence**. Some put a high premium upon the acquisition of money or material goods. Others only want enough to eke out an existence.

S stands for **Structure.** Some need rigid structure, and everything in its place. Others seem to destroy structure just by walking into a room.

I stands for **Interaction.** There are those whose work suffers if they are not able to interact with others. Their opposites are distracted by people.

C stands for **Control**. Some people need to control their world and the people in it. Others will take drastic measures to avoid that power.

Outlined above are the extremes on the values scale. Most of us fall somewhere between in positions noted. However, it is important to understand the value structure of your business or company and select employees whose basic values blend with corporate values.

It is important to understand each other's values, for when they are violated, clashes occur. For example, Elizabeth once worked for an individual who had no doubt that those he hired would do their job, be innovative, work well with each other, and relate well with the customers. However, he was compulsive about time, and every morning he prowled the halls to make certain that each manager was in his or her office, not just on time, but 30 minutes early. Those who weren't there at least 30 minutes early, he considered to lack dedication and be poor team players. There was no point in telling this person that their day began at 8:00 a.m., for he believed that the managers' day never stopped. He was always in at 6:00 a.m. and identified best with those who had the same drive and energy level.

Since this is important to him, it needs to be noted in every job description for those who report directly to him.

In addition, every job description should describe how the employee will have to relate to the customers and what is expected to ensure that the best possible service is given.

- **Switchboard Operators** know they are front line, but they sometimes forget this critical information:
    - their tone of voice is vital
    - their enunciation patterns must be clear
    - the first two words they speak are "throw aways" and people often miss them
    - they should never say, "Will you wait," and then not wait for an answer
    - 28 seconds is as long as someone should ever be left on hold
    - a smile helps even over the phone
    - unplugging at 5:00 p.m. sharply is **never** justified if anyone is still on the line.
- **Maintenance Personnel** should be told how important they are to the company's image and

reminded that:

- the gardener's work has tremendous impact
- fresh paint makes a good first impression
- restroom conditions have an immediate impact
- trash baskets should be emptied and cleaned regularly
- desks and furniture need to be dusted frequently
- windows should be clean
- parking lots should be clean and weedless
- plants should be watered regularly
- and upholstered furniture should be cleaned on a regular basis.

Every position is a customer-contact job directly or indirectly, and the job description needs to spell this out. Accountants need to remember that bills should arrive at their destination close to the same date every month, that checks should be cut for purchases within the time frame set by the company, and that errors should not be blamed on computer error. Of course, you still need to list the job qualifications as you do today, but you also need to go beyond that to behaviors and customer service expectations.

> **"Draegers, an upscale grocery in Menlo Park, California, has enjoyed a 57% growth in sales over the past three years by combining the convenience of a modern supermarket with old-fashioned service."**
>
> ***NATION'S BUSINESS***

ADVERTISING THE JOB

Happy employees often attract good applicants, and many companies never even get to the job flyer or advertisement stage. Many companies, such as Delta Airlines, provide their own employees with opportunities to "try out" other positions in order to broaden their skills base. When you advertise, make certain that it incorporates the following:

- human expectations
- key words for the behavioral style wanted
- the benefits—beyond money and fringes

Let's try it. Here is a job opening for a senior analyst. The job requires someone who is detailed, able to work on precision based problems, alone or with a small staff. In addition, the person needs to be one who is steady, stable, and follows through. That person has certain key words and phrases that will make a job appeal to him/her—team player, dedicated, solve problems, support, and security.

Advertisement One:

Well-established company seeks experienced analyst to assist in department charged with data gathering for the engineering department of a major real estate firm based in the Valley. This person will be responsible for maintaining current systems, chairing the proposal committee, and supervising and evaluating a staff of four. A minimum of three years experience is required, and the person must be able to write proposals. Business experience required, M.B.A. preferred.

Advertisement Two:

We need a team player who is willing to work with a team of four to gather data and maintain

> our current engineering systems. Our ten-year-old company is growing and needs dedicated, innovative people interested in growing with us and able to solve computer related problems. We'll provide support and security if your talents match our needs.

Which of the advertisements above will attract the applicant you want? Number one is in the traditional mode, but number two is designed to appeal to your ideal candidate!

> **Write your advertisements and job flyers in behavioral terms to appeal to those who match.**

Tell the truth, be honest, inventive, and describe what really happens on that job. If you have a sales job open, it will need to be drafted quite differently from the advertisement that goes out of an engineering position. The person you want may need to be fast-paced, inventive, undaunted by a challenge, people-oriented, enthusiastic, energetic, and willing to tackle problems without any precedents to go by. Say it clearly in your advertisement!

Advertisement Three:

> Ready for a real challenge? Interested in meeting people? Tired of having an earnings cap? Then this is the job for you. Our two-year-old company is in a growth mode and adding to our sales force. We need someone who isn't a clock watcher to take over an untried territory and build it. We will pay a small base, cover expenses, and set up a sliding scale commission structure. Interested? Call us at ...

WIDEN THE SEARCH

The same companies that will scour the countryside for business, spend thousands advertising their products/services, and join every organization in town, will call a placement agency and then **just wait** for the right candidate to be sent over. Did it ever occur to you that the **right candidate** may not be waiting in the wings for your job offer?

Be as innovative in seeking employees as you are in seeking business.

- network
- contact associations and professional organizations

- talk to colleagues and ask for recommendations

- meet with the agency recruiters and give an in-depth description of your firm

  - its mission
  - its working philosophy
  - its values
  - its goals
  - and the background and behaviors needed in the job you are offering

- put the word out among your own employees

- go to trade shows and meet people

- ask for names of people in other companies

This all takes time, but so does staff turnover.

THE INTERVIEW PROCESS

Once the applicants start appearing, you need to have your interviewing plans in place. Many people rely on only the 5W's and 1H approach to interviewing:

- Where did you work last?

- How long were you there?

- What was your degree in?
- When will you be ready to begin a new job?
- Why are you changing jobs just now?
- Who can give us information about your experience and capabilities?

If you stopped there, you probably missed out on a great deal of information. Let's do some planning. List what you want this person to do, the characteristics and skills that are important in this job. Rank them. What values are important to you and need to be important to the new employee? Now—set up practical situations and go from there.

- Outline something that might happen in your organization that would pose a problem related to following rules. Ask the person how he/she would handle it. You can learn what comes first—rules or customers.
- You can either have the candidate take a values assessment instrument such as VALUES CHECK which we use, or find out some of the motivators by just asking. (See the RBASIC list).
- Ask the person to state his/her greatest strength, weakness.

- Ask where the person expects to be in five years, as far as his/her career is concerned.

- Ask what he/she admires most in a leader, and in a good colleague.

Vary the way you direct these questions. Some should be open-ended, some leading, some direct, some should require the person to respond with a vignette, and some a combination of these. For example:

Leading Question: What did you admire most about your last boss, and what did you learn from working for this person?

Vignette: What would you do to help an employee who has poor interpersonal skills? Perhaps you can tell me about a past situation of a similar nature and how you dealt with it.

Open-ended: You must have some questions about this position. What would you like to know?

Luck plays little, or no role, in good staffing, and when asked what they valued in good employees—those they would consider for advancement—executives responding to a *Wall Street Journal* questionnaire identified the following traits:

- good communication skills
- integrity
- dedication
- empathy
- decision making skills
- enthusiasm
- the ability to build rapport
- honesty

Plan your interview questions so that you draw out information related to these areas, e.g. "In your last job I see that you worked alone much of the time. Are you comfortable or happiest when you can work on projects without others around?"

Make the interview fun!

Interviews shouldn't be stressful for you or the candidates. Put them at ease, establish rapport with them—mirror—and introduce yourself and the others who are with you by both name and title. Smile, keep a pleasant tone, and look at the candidates.

Don't set it up like a trial—all of you on one side of a desk or table and the candidate opposite on the other side. One of us remembers an interview that would have made a congressional hearing look relaxed. The candidate walked into a board room which had fixed theater style chairs facing a raised area upon which was a curved desk area with seven large, high-backed chairs behind it. Each position had a flexible mike stand in front of it, and every seat in the room was vacant. The candidate was told to take a seat in the middle of the front row and wait for the panel to convene. Fifteen minutes elapsed with only the clock providing any sound. Then six somber men entered the room, filed behind the desks, sat down, opened their briefcases, took out materials, and looked sternly across at the person to be interviewed. **Trial—trial—trial**—were the words that rushed through the candidate's mind. The interview was off to a **negative** beginning. An interview is not a hearing and should not be structured like one if you really want to learn more about the "real" person being interviewed.

We're all here for the interview, now what?

Gather data! The information on the application can be expanded upon here. If the person has participated in a number of organizations and has assumed leadership roles in all of them, you are getting a powerful message about the person's ability to assume authority and the level of the value related to control.

Appearance and eye contact will give you additional messages. Dress will tell you which drummer they step to and how. Gestures and pace of speaking will give you a great deal more information.The person who is speaking fast may be nervous, but more than likely that is a results oriented person who wants to get things done, get to the bottom of a problem, and deal with it directly.

The candidate is not the only one being interviewed—you are, too! Selection interviews should be two-way communication. If you did your homework, studied the job, defined it properly, wrote the job description and advertisement properly, then you are at the stage where most of the inappropriate candidates have already screened themselves out of the picture. Those who will be in this final group are here because they see this as a chance that fits them and offers them an opportunity for success.

Broaden the scope of the interview.

Take them on a tour, pause and introduce them to others. Particularly introduce them to those in positions similar to the one for which they are interviewing. Let them meet some of those with whom they will be working, if hired.

Office conditions affect people differently. The applicant needs to see how offices are laid out, how close people have to sit, the level of noise, and the general tone/ambiance of the office. If his/her reaction is negative, you are better off knowing it at this stage than later after you have dismissed all the other candidates.

If possible, let the person go out alone to talk to some of your employees or leave them alone for a few minutes with some of them. The applicant will be in a better position to know if this is a fit or not after being exposed to the workplace and the people in it.

> **"We as managers have a responsibility to improve the quality of our people as well as our product."**
>
> **Dustan Goodell**
> **Resident Manager**
> **Worthington Hotel**

An increasing number of companies are setting up their versions of the mock trials used to test law students. "Real life situations" are set up and "real work stations" are used to introduce the applicant to possible situations and see how the person would perform. Their responses are then judged in a far more valid way than could ever be done from just questions during an interview.

- A computer programmer is put into a station where the system "has gone down" and asked to get it up and running.

- A managerial candidate is put on stage with some actors and they "play act" a pre-set scene before a video camera—later reviewing and discussing the results.

- Five-day "interviews" are set up by having the person come and "try the job on for size" for five days.

Some companies are setting peer panels which generally are used at the initial screening stages. Other companies are now having the last two or three candidates appear before a peer panel constituted of most of those with whom they will work. We know of one organization that even brings in some of its top clients for the last screening step. When these panels are used, those serving and those they represent seem to feel that they have an "ownership" in the selection. When the person they select is hired, they all have a vested interest in helping the person succeed. If, on the other hand, the person they do not select is brought in, there is often resentment. The panel members may well feel that they wasted their time and were ignored or thwarted.

AND THEN?

If you have used formal ratings sheets;

- interview reports have been filled out,
- skills tests have been evaluated,
- and paperwork has been scored,

then you are ready to decide. If you find that your expectations are met at an 80% level, you have found your employee. Make the offer to the top candidate right away and let the others know immediately. Gossip is often faster than any other media. Don't let the applicants hear by the "grapevine." Thank them for their interest, and leave the door open.

There are times when company or organizational policy have limitations that are not considered in the preceding pages. Live by them, and begin to seek changes that will make it possible to have more latitude in the future. Government change is often slow, but no less slow than that in some companies.The effort will be worth it once the change is in place.

**Hire today for tomorrow
and change
as the market changes.**

6

THE DEADLY SINS OF CUSTOMER SERVICE

"Customer satisfaction can only be achieved when you effectively communicate, communicate, and communicate with your customer. You can never overdo this aspect of your business. Also, communication is a two-way street—you need to hear as much as you say."

D. J. Zolkiwsky
Technical Business Operations Director
A.T. & T. Bell Laboratories

The real sin in business comes in multiples of six. It seems illogical, but we only have to spend a day in the marketplace to see that. The customer is a nuisance to many, not an asset. Every service we offer, every product we sell, every idea we wish to market must have a customer, and most businesses need repeat customers and referrals in order to succeed. So, let's take a look at the deadly sixes—the quicksands that pull us down unless we are vigilent.

You set the goals you get.

The first set of deadly sins, and all the others, only exist as long as we permit them. **Remember, you always get exactly what you want—if you say you can, you can; if you say you can't, you can't.!** That means that it is up to you—management and staff—to make certain that customers never encounter

- **Disinterest or boredom.** At a local DMV office, someone leaned down and picked up a scarf off the floor. She looked around, didn't see anyone who appeared to be looking for it, headed to a nearby counter to ask for directions to the lost and found department. The woman at the counter looked up, bored and annoyed, and said, "If you want information, go over to that line." The person who found the scarf looked at the line, moved over to it and after ten minutes shrugged in disgust, tossed the scarf on a bench and left. It took the employee as long to redirect the woman as it would have taken to help, but her harsh tone, rude manner, and glower turned off the "good Samaritan." Now for a little irony. About fifteen minutes later, the same bored, disinterested employee told a nearby colleague that she had lost a scarf that had been tied to her handbag. The one found may or many not have been her's, but she'll never know.

- **"That's not my job."** A service-driven company's employees realize that the customer is everyone's job—they run the company;they pay the bills.

> **"That's Not My Job"**
>
> **This is a story about four people named Everybody, Somebody, Anybody and Nobody. There was an important job to be done and Everybody was sure that Somebody would do it. Anybody could have done it, but Nobody did it. Somebody got angry about that, because it was Everybody's job. Everybody thought Anybody could do it, but Nobody realized that Everybody wouldn't do it. It ended up that Everybody blamed Somebody when Nobody did what Anybody could have.**
>
> **— Anonymous**

- **Hautiness.** Have you every wondered why the person you encounter first in many establishments seems to have been selected to drive you away? Consider the sales clerk whose entire attitude is geared to letting you know how minimal is your value as a customer or the nurse who tells you that "the doctor" is busy even though you have been waiting 50 minutes—45 minutes past your appointment.

- **A missing person**. We know that humanoids exist only in books, or do they? The business world seems to have a large number of Stepfordites out there giving us—"thank you-have a good day" with vacant eyes above glued-on smiles.

- **It's our policy**. When the rule book left it out or when the rule book says no, all too often there is no recourse for the average patron. Only recently have banks begun to accommodate patrons by permitting them to cancel payment on checks without coming into the branch where their account is located. Several years ago, a problem arouse about a check accidently torn in two, one of the authors was in New York and her bank was in Los Angeles. The vendor wanted the check replaced. Four tries and the only result—"You must come in to the bank and make the request in person." Even the offer of a notarized request was denied. Thank heavens that such rigidity is being reconsidered by most service establishments, who now realize that they "don't have the only game in town."

- **Pass the buck.** "I'm so sorry, I don't handle that." "Oh, I wish I could help, but that is not my department, let me transfer you, or I'll tell him when he gets back from vacation next month."

These might be funny in an old Laurel and Hardy movie, but they occur far too often for us to even want to see them in real life anymore. Keep a diary for the next ten days—which of these sins do you encounter or see occurring? List them. Then, play detective at your own business—are many of them occuring there? Now discuss the situation with your staff, and do a little strategic planning on ways you can work together to avoid them.

> "Customer relations that are based on analyzing customer complaints will never provide world class results. To be effective, customer relations need to be based on profound knowledge of the customer's needs and the needs of his/her customer. The result is to provide for the customer without waiting for a complaint."
>
> Joseph P. Broz
> Vice President
> James River Corporation

THE SIX DEADLY SINS

Disinterest or boredom

"That's not my job."

Haughtiness

A Missing Person

"It's our policy."

Pass the buck

Points to Remember

A rose by any other name is still a rose, and poor service no matter what you say is still poor service. It doesn't matter what your advertisements say if the customer doesn't recognize your service or product when they see it.

We've been tempted to "sample buy" a number of frozen foods and see how closely they resemble the pictures on the packages or in the ads. You can show me a Maxim meal and call it "quality dining," but a limp meatloaf, grey-green beans, and watery pudding only tells me you think I'm either near-sighted or stupid. Those ads, those slogans, those rote greetings don't improve my reaction nor the service, but they may well create cynics. **Advertise only what you can and will deliver."**

- **New is not always better.** The automobile industry builds into its planning, annual body changes and assumes that it must do so in order to keep and attract buyers. Now a strange thing is happening. Car builders are making fortunes recreating the styles that major automotive companies deemed obsolete. The "VW Beetle" is still sought after, and if a Gull Wing were reintroduced it would probably sell again as well or even better, than it did when it was on the market. Maytag has built an entire advertising campaign around its dependability—and that bored, underworked repairman has become synonymous with dependability and quality.

- **Cost is more important than service.** Tell that to the thousands of boutiques that have effectively undermined the client base of their large sister stores. Tell that to the Mercedes dealers. Tell that to Nordstroms.

- **More is better.** Like inexpensive clothing which often seems to have more decoration, more yardage, and more color, some vendors seem to think the "packing" is the way to best serve. Advertisements are overcrowded and try to fit in every piece of information available; aisles are close, congested, and overflowing; seating is crowded—shoulder to shoulder and knee to knee; and brochures try to tell everything in one paragraph, or worse yet dozen of paragraphs.

- **Customer comments without change.** Hotels put a little white card on your dresser. Restaurants put a comment card near the salt. Department stores send out questionnaires. Some of us dutifully fill out these suggestion cards and happily, some of the businesses actually read them, and act on the suggestions. Unfortunately, many just collect them, compile the information, and use the input as a general guideline, not pinpointing specific items, as the base for planning or change. Slogans get changed instead of behaviors.

- **Platitudes have meaning.** The polite "Thank you" tells you nothing. The question, "How did you enjoy your visit, stay, or trip?", is generally answered by polite responses—some people will tell you the negatives—but unless you ask specific questions, you won't learn how it could have been improved and made more attractive to them and others like them.

- **They know we will pay**. Things get tight, accountants get busy, payment dates slip by, and you know that your vendors—who are customers in another sense—know you well enough to understand. Nonsense, that's their money, not yours. Once a vendor has provided the product, service, or idea, he or she has earned the money. It is not yours to hold, and certainly not to "float." It may be economically desirable to control that money a little longer, but it is not worth your reputation or the negative public relations that result.

The Stations of Success

One:	A pre-planned strategy
Two:	Quality
Three:	Service-driven front line
Four:	Supportive management
Five:	Sound hiring procedures
Six:	Effective supervision
Seven:	Evaluation and a willingness to change

7

WAYS TO MONITOR CUSTOMER SERVICE

"Never promise what you can't deliver and never assume that you can unless you measure the results!"

T.S. Eliot once said that the world will end not with a bang but a whimper. This might well describe the collapse of a business. No fanfare accompanies its death, few mourners are to be seen, and like an "old general," it just fades away.

Companies that grow and prosper seem to have one thing in common—a well-established, multifaceted data gathering network. When you set up a specific process and seek specific information, you will get rid of the "never" and "always" syndrome. People aren't

always happy with the service and/or product, nor do they **never** complain. Such sweeping assessments provide false information, and you can't build on sand.

GATHERING THE DATA

There are a number of steps that need to be taken to insure that you have all the information needed to monitor effectively.

Taking your company's pulse.

- **Ask your customers about your service or product**. (Hotels, restaurants, shops, and even the DMV have questionnaires placed in obvious locations and request feedback.) Design a questionnaire that fits your company and use it.

> **"The guest is king, so give him what he wants and give it to him at a fair price."**
>
> **William N. Hultee**
> **President**
> **Stouffer Hotel Company**

- **Try your company's service "on for size."** One restaurant owner in Newport Beach, California, dresses casually and then walks up to his restaurant as if he were debating whether to go in or not. He waits until someone comes out and asks if it is a good place to eat and if the service is good. He gathers any other details they will share. After several interchanges, he has a pretty good idea of his restaurant's rating in the minds of that evening's customers.

- **Use a mystery shopper service.** Let them place orders, stay for a night, request help, call in for information, etc. There are many companies whose services have paid dividends far in excess of the fee charged. Two of the authors own such a service and number among their clients such diverse businesses as the Embassy Suites, Affiliated Food, and MacDonald's. The system works because a good service provides specifics that can be used to evaluate, plan, and take corrective action. [The next chapter will deal more extensively with the process.]

- **Encourage feedback.** In a study conducted in the late 1970's for the Federal Office of Consumer Affairs, only 54.3 percent of those who complained and got satisfaction said they would go back to the same vendor. You can't provide satisfaction if you don't know what went wrong.

WAYS TO MONITOR CUSTOMER SERVICE

- **Design and conduct a survey.** If your company fits into the guidelines, there are even government grants that can be tapped for this purpose, You can use the information to help you prioritize more appropriately.

- **Be logical.** When you hear only silence out there, get busy. Customers are not that quiet unless they are leaving. According to Linda Silverman Goldzimer, the author of I'M FIRST, "For every five complaints received, there are a hundred problem products (or services) out there." Now follow her one more step and remember that every dissatisfied customer is likely to tell another eleven people. If there are a hundred problems out there, then "1,100 people are hearing that your product is no good." She calls this phenomenon the Iceberg Factor, because what you hear is really only the tip of the problem.

- **Shop your competitors.** Travel on those other airlines. Eat in those other restaurants. Order products, use them, and evaluate them. Be objective—what do they have to offer that you don't? How does their service or product compare to yours—specifically and honestly? Once you have those answers, you can look at yours with an eye toward improvement—product, service, and publicity.

- **Mingle.** Two of the authors worked with the Marriott Corporation and designed their OPTS program on hospitality. During their site research period, they learned that it is the hotel's policy to have managers mingle, greet, and ask. Mingle so that the patrons know that someone is in charge and cares; greet to establish rapport and put people at ease; and ask questions in order to get vital feedback that will provide input for strategy planning sessions.

- **Be objective**. Take a long look at your performance and the performance of your competitors. What is their image and why? Where and what do you have to improve and change? Don't fix it if it works, but be alert and take action when it is time to change.

- **Be practical.** Eliminate service and products that don't appeal or matter to your clients. Don't set goals that raise costs to the point that you are no longer competitive in time or cost.

- **Take the initiative**. When there is a problem, when there is a personality clash, or when there are errors, don't sit back and hope that everything will work out. Go to your client, explain that you feel dedicated to produce the best possible level of work or provide the best possible level of service, and are concerned about the problem that has occurred. Ignoring the problem has two negative aspects—it can lose a customer, and a repetition of the situation can cost you another one later. It is up to you to learn what happened, correct it, and make certain that it doesn't happen again.

Many of us have been in relationships where we knew something was wrong, but we were afraid to ask questions. We were fearful that we would find out what it was and would be unable to fix it. This same attitude is carried into the workplace, and many salespeople and managers tell us that they aren't sure what is wrong. They know something is, but if they don't know they can't fix it. If this is the attitude of your staff, then it is imperative that you design and put into place some training programs specifically tailored to help them deal more effectively with such a situation. These programs should include

- specific information about products, services, rules, regulations, and decision-making powers
- identification of common problems
- problem-solving and strategic planning

- training on how to "read" and interact with people
- opportunities to role play in a non-threatening environment
- feedback, support, and follow-up reinforcement.

FEEDBACK COMES IN VARIOUS FORMS

The comment cards that appear on desktops and hotel dressers will give you information on one or two incidents within a tight time frame. But, you will have to use these cards for a prolonged period before they give you an overview of any magnitude or value. In addition, the format of the comment cards may hinder your data gathering process. Often they look like elementary school report cards—excellent, good, satisfactory, poor. When you get these cards, stockpile them, read and tabulate, what did you learn? **How they felt about your service and products,** but not **why**. Isn't **"why"** the crucial question? Was phone etiquette poor, lighting inadequate, or the food cold? Who knows, you certainly don't and can't from those cards unless you ask.

WAYS TO MONITOR CUSTOMER SERVICE

Your questionnaire needs to be specifically related to what you want to know:

- Can you provide a variety of banking services? Did the manager tell the new depositor about them?

- Are you considering a new phone system? When the customer called in did he/she have to wait on the line or go through several people before reaching the right person?

If you think some services or systems need to be added or deleted, then find out. When you change approaches, alter policies, design guidelines, monitor, train and support, you will see change. Remember, in every dance the leader sets the pace and pattern, and the follower responds. Change the step and the dance has to change.

> **"For every problem there is a solution."**
>
> **H. L. Mencken**

Do not, we repeat, do not trigger negatives that aren't there. Some questionnaires have a section that asks what don't you like about this product or service. We resolved never to use that item again after one person told us that it had been the hardest item to fill-in since he really had liked everything. He searched and searched until he finally found a negative, just because we asked for one. But once written down, we had no way of knowing that it wasn't reflecting his real concern.

You may consider phrasing your questions like this:

- What were the strengths (merits) of this product (service) from your point of view?

- Is there anything you would like to see changed or added?

- How are you using the information (product) to enhance your own business (performance)?

- What has helped you (what do you value) the most?

- Would you recommend this product (service) to others? Why? Do you have someone in particular you would like us to contact? If so, jot their name and address/phone number below, and we will be happy to do so.

You can probe for quality, usefulness, suggestions, satisfaction, and referrals in a very short space.

What else can you do? Here is a Feedback Checklist.

FEEDBACK CHECKLIST

Have you checked:

_____ customer complaints or tracked them to determine a pattern?

_____ with your sales people for feedback?

_____ with your phone staff for feedback?

_____ the copies of all complaint letters?

_____ randomly, the survey calls placed to customers/clients?

_____ community involvement levels? Are you represented in various organizations?

_____ complaint response time—not what is said, what is done?

_____ to make certain that your staff approaches problems positively?

_____ to see if your staff is taking steps to relieve or correct the problem?

_____ to see how long customers are kept on hold?

_____ to see if customers are the losers in telephone "pass-around?"

_____ to make certain that all your staff has had appropriate training. Is there a way to ensure that new hires are brought up to equal levels of performance with those who have had specific training?

_____ to make certain that employees who perform well on a consistent basis are rewarded verbally and via appropriate incentives?

_____ to make certain that problems are handled with style? *

* A well-known strategist, Pete Johnson, once said that "when the disagreeable becomes the inevitable, do it with style."

A restaurant owner in New Orleans puts this view into action. One hot and humid evening, a number of us stood outside his restaurant waiting to get in. The wait was to have been 15 minutes, but time seemed to be standing still. He defused the growing anger and hostility by coming out, going up and down the line and asking each person what he or she would like to have to drink while they waited, and then he added the "style," an entertainer was sent out to keep our spirits up and a waitress walked up and down the line offering each person a choice of various cheeses and crackers.

Another restaurant, the Cheese and Olive Cafe in Marina del Rey, California, puts a card at each table telling customers that "our staff works as a team in order to better serve you. You need not look for the person who initially took your order for additional service, just ask anyone!" By putting "everyone on (their) staff" on alert to serve their customers, they provide quicker, more efficient service, spot needs and meet them more effectively, and are building a stronger customer base than are many of their competitors.

TAKE A TIP FROM THE POLITICIANS

Politicians get to know their constituents by attending **Coffee Klatches**. Why not set up something of that nature in your offices or at a local restaurant? Encourage people to talk freely, and have your staff invite those who have been the most supportive and who have voiced some concerns. You will get a real cross-section if you do it right and a good picture of what is really going on from the customer's point of view.

Go to the sites, talk to people, and if you want to use what you learn as part of a training program, see if you can set up some cameras and video tape the interviews. Ask those interviewed what they like best about the product or service, what they like least, and what they would like to see happen to make this the "best" of its kind. Edit and polish the video—edit for quality not content—and build some training sessions around it. This approach worked well for the Marriot Corporation, and the finished video was sent to all General Managers for use with their staffs.

Don't screen the calls. When you put layers and layers between you and your "constituents—customers" you have almost guaranteed that you will be the last to know what is working and what is floundering. And never let your staff answer the phone this way

> "Good morning, Mr. Readi's office. Could I tell him who's calling? Thank you. Let me see if he's in."

Most people assume that you are screening calls and will only accept certain ones—they are frequently insulted. This would have been acceptable with minor changes.

> "Good morning, Mr. Readi's office. I'm not certain he's in, but if he is, could I tell him who's calling? Thank you.

The President of SeaPac in Seattle insists that his executives answer their own phone whenever possible. When it is not possible, those who do answer are instructed to tell the caller where the person is and promise to give him or her the message ASAP (as soon as possible). At no time is a staff person permitted to ask the name of the caller—you may find this too extreme—in order to insure that the person does not feel screened.

SHORTEN THE INFORMATION LOOP

Open your own door. Take the open door policy one more step outward and get out into the customers world. Contact some of your clients and go to their places of business. See how

- your product is being used
- your service is being received
- your training program is being implemented.

Before you even offer the service or product, check with some of their branches (if any) and ask specific questions about needs, uses, problems, etc. Then your staff will be in a better position to provide assistance, back up, and information.

A loss can be a win if you use it right. Call a client who went to a competitor for a service or product. Find out why. If it is something you can change—and want to change—then take action. For example, when we don't get contracts, we call the client and ask them to help us learn more about services we can provide effectively. We politely inquire about the reasons for the choice made and how that product or service differed from what we offered. We have learned a great deal from this type of informal survey. Sometimes we go back to the drawing board and map out new directions; in other instances we leave things as they are—i.e., pricing.

To each his own view. Remember the story of the elephant and the three blind men? The first thought the creature was long and skinny after he ran his hands down the trunk. The second was certain that the animal was soft and very flexible after he has felt the ears, and the third knew that this was something that was stocky and very solid—he had felt the leg. The message—don't take just one person's reaction as the base for change. Years ago, we had the audacity to bring a bright red electric typewriter into the office. The secretary loved it—the color made her feel good. The maintenance department hated it. She was always calling them to come out to fix a spring that kept flying off into the air, and one of the clerks avoided it because it had too many "gadgets" on it. One typewriter, three points of view. You can't afford to have a narrow survey.

Go direct. At the end of each seminar or program we offer, we ask for an evaluation, and many of our clients use a similar approach. They send the new customer or client a card asking them to evaluate the product and service. Did they like it? Did they get courteous, prompt service? Is the product or service all that they anticipated? If you decide to do this, keep it short, have brief questions and spaces for them to fill-in, and pre-stamp and address the return envelope.

Use the data. No one likes to have their time wasted. While they may waste it, they don't welcome your doing it. That means that you need to use the results of your surveys, questionnaires, interviews, meetings, and

- analyze the information
- identify trends, if any
- look for causes
- find communalities and see what categories they fall under. Many problems are closely related and part of a bigger picture. It is far better to deal with the "big picture" rather than the parts.

- consider the cost of not changing and the cost—and resulting profit—of changing

- how does this impact upon staff now—if you change?

- how extensive will the ripple be? Will the disruption be worth it?

You also need to share the information gleaned with the staff. The more closely involved and informed they are, the more they will support changes and produce as a team.

Tap internal talent and data sources. Bring together representatives from various departments and have them brainstorm.

Step One: Brainstorm and have each group list all that is going on that makes your company or organization "great" and could be the base for good public relations. Use a flip chart to record the responses. Remove the individual pages and post them around the room.

Step Two: Take a coffee break and let people walk around and look at the posted "brag sheets." They will feel good, and you have the base for the next step—matching "haves" to "needs."

Step Three: Make a chart on the flip chart and divide it in half vertically. Head one side "Customer Needs" and the other "Company Pluses."

Under "Customer Needs", list all that you have learned from surveys, interviews, mail, etc. Now go into the next column, "Company Pluses". Using the "Plus" column, list the products/services you offer which match the customer "Need". You are in good shape if for every "Need" there is a "Plus". If there is a gap, you need to determine why your product/service does not fill the "Need", and how to correct the problem. If you walk away from the gaps, you can just keep on walking—away from business.

Make it a team effort. Use those staff meetings to discuss, plan, and problem solve. In order for this to work, there must be an atmosphere conducive to total candor. You staff must feel free to tell all—positive and negative—without fear of reprisals. This means that the barriers, if any, between staff and management must come down. Just remember that the employees are the management's customers and the management is the employees' customer. If either group knows that the other can't take bad news, becomes upset when negatives are mentioned, or takes conveyed criticism/

feedback as personal affronts, then the feedback will stop. If it stops, you and the company are the losers for vital information will be withheld.

Create a Customer Team. Call it an Advisory Panel or Customer Board, and get them involved in your company and its planning and feedback strategies. Let them review advertising, job flyers, logos, and projections. Make certain that they realize that it is input not directives that you want. Make certain that you let them know that the time they spend and the information they share are appreciated. Do something tangible to show that appreciation. Since people—volunteers included—like to have a sense of belonging and a sense of responsibility, divide up the responsibilities. Give each one specific responsibilities and take their input seriously. When their services are recognized, be sure to remember and mention their area of responsibility.

If you will use the techniques and suggestions outlined in this chapter, you will be able to preplan instead of react. Feedback is frequently sought **after** the problems have surfaced. It needs to be collected **before** problems occur, in an organized and on-going manner. If you don't know the problem exists, you certainly can't solve it, nor can you measure success if you haven't identified the benchmarks that lead to it.

8

MYSTERY SHOPPING: Another way to monitor

"Customers rarely give second chances. The most accurate way to find out how your customers perceive your business is mystery shopping. When it comes to your customers, no news is not necessarily good news."

Barbra Anderson and Mary Jo Tellin
Co-Founders of
Search for Excellence, Inc.

You may hire a mystery shopper. There are a number of companies that will "shop" for you and provide detailed, well-documented reports about what they found. Two of the authors run such a company, and as part of their service to industry they

- anonymously audit customer service and look
- at first impressions
- product knowledge

    - customer treatment
    - salesmanship
    - manner

- provide a form of market research that can be applied to any kind of business as long as it has customers, clients, patrons, and/or members.

Throughout the country hundreds of well-trained "shoppers" are dining out, checking into hotels, making purchases, calling in for information, even opening bank accounts as a means of gaining first hand knowledge about customer service. Companies hire these market researchers because they want to

- learn more about their customers' needs
- evaluate current programs, performance, and situations
- monitor new programs—training, customer service or promotional
- build the staff's awareness of the importance of customer service to a service-driven industry.

Luckily, there is no bad time to start. This isn't a seasonal project, but it is vital to remember that it is a cost effective three-part undertaking, combining

- data gathering
- planning for change or reinforcement
- and acting.

Based upon what is learned during the "shopping spree," companies can target areas needing improvement, and since the reports include specific information about needs, suggestions for incentives, and recommendations for establishing on-going training, companies can take giant steps in short time periods. The information gleaned by such shoppers provides the basis for a game plan for bringing about the changes needed.

If you decide to hire "mystery shoppers," make certain that you select a firm that offers a turn-key package that is customer-tailored to your company. That customizing is essential to insuring that you get the results that make the difference. One thing you can be sure of—there is no standard report. Sometimes the results are hilarious, often surprising, and occasionally horrid.

What "shoppers" often find is "mediocre service—not too bad and not too good...people just go through the motions." One of the advantages of using "shoppers" rather than depending solely upon supervisors' reports is pointed out by Elisha Miller, manager of in-flight performance for United Airlines. "It is human nature...if people know they are being watched, they change their behavior...We want an accurate reading of how the customer in the real world perceives our performance."

In order to be successful in their work, shoppers must be "someone we would expect to encounter there." Once a shopper is identified, they can no longer return to that location—they have served their purpose and must be replaced. Who are those shoppers—your neighbors! Grandparents, doctors, lawyers, teachers, clerks, station attendants, mechanics, builders—everyone and anyone may be a shopper, but they all have one thing in common, careful training. They are taught to

- audit first impressions
- note product knowledge
- check out the parking
- note appearance
- see if signs are in place
- evaluate the product
- note time-lapse before greeting
- note type of greeting
- grade on attitude

- check on smile-levels
- evaluate exterior appearance
- evaluate salesmanship
- evaluate follow-through
- grade on eagerness
- evaluate internal appearance
- check ambiance

In an article that appeared in February, 1989, in the Restaurant Association's publication, it was noted that the "most important part of marketing...is customer service." Since 67% of the people who try a new restaurant do so because of... word-of-mouth advertising," it is important to keep that service up. "People don't recommend restaurants with poor service."

The article went on to note that "one way to ensure that a restaurant markets itself is through checking food and service through mystery shopping." By using this service, problems can be eliminated early, and clients who use the service have noted increases in revenue and customer satisfaction. Even small businesses can afford to use this service. "Mom and Pop stores would be able to learn something, too— low-cost, easy-to-implement suggestions that fit their budgets."

Dick Huiras of Humark Management in Houston pointed out that "we stressed that our servers were salespeople" working on commissions (their tips). Once they understood that, it was amazing "how the employees could build check averages—market, if you will."

One of the things that is often skipped in the evaluation process is the impact of design—design is packaging and as such it attracts the visually oriented person. It is also important to note both internal and external design—the outside may get them in, but the food and the interior decor will keep them coming back. A good shopper will make note of these things, too, for the information is helpful when the market report is prepared.

The sophistication level of the suggestions can make the executive's job easier. How can we attract customers—suggested approaches need to be tailored to the market target. A family restaurant does well via direct mail with discount coupons designed to get them in to try it. An upscale one would be wiser to buy some radio time because their clientele will be trapped in that morning and afternoon traffic listening to the radio.

In essence, those hiring shoppers are really seeking advice from their customers in a direct and very reliable way.

The columnist, Charles Bernstein, is right when he says "Quality food and a winning menu may be the ingredients that initially attracts customers. But friendly service and a genuine smile will ... keep them coming back."

> "To survive in today's marketplace, it is essential that we go back to the old fashioned approach of knowing your business, your customer or guest, and *for sure* your competition...these are critical elements to success and the foundation for providing quality services."
>
> Antonio C. Luna
> Senior Vice President
> Club Resorts, Inc.

MYSTERY SHOPPING IS A WINNING PROCESS

Like every other successful undertaking, the process of mystery shopping has a definite structure and pattern. For example, a hotel manager might want help in identifying the reason for a decline in reservations. A "mystery guest" would be dispatched and begin the evaluation with the initial call for reservations.

- Was the phone answered promptly?
- Was the greeting friendly?
- Were the reservations processed quickly?

Other matters will be evaluated after the "mystery guest" arrives.

- What is the overall physical condition and appearance of the hotel?
- What were the front desk procedures?

Even before the "mystery guest" gets into the room, the shoppers (at least those employed by the Dallas-based company, Search for Excellence) will have evaluated the hotel on some 518 points, and before they finish the visit, some 6,792 other points will have been evaluated, including

- room service
- housekeeping
- the restaurant
- the bar
- special facilities
- and especially check-out.

The report will be unbiased and may give data not only on the points of initial interest but also on some unexpected ones. In fact, many times, they turn up a problem or an example of outstanding service, something that hadn't even been suspected or realized.

SHOP YOUR COMPETITION!

Who says that it's a secret? Who says you can't find out what your competition is up to? There are some easy, legal, and inexpensive ways to find out what they are doing, and you can even use shoppers to help you get that information, if you want to.

Secrets are worth money—if your competitor is introducing a new product, cutting prices, relocating, or expanding, you need to know. Obviously, you can't—and wouldn't—bug board rooms, bribe employees, or steal patents, but there are some very ethical ways of finding out what your are up against. Arrange to have mystery shoppers

- Visit your competitor's place of business and evaluate it just as you do yours.

- "Hang out" in common areas near the competitor's place of business. Fascinating information is often shared freely enough that diners at nearby tables hear easily.

  We learned in a restaurant at a convention that one of our competitors was planning to bring out a book on the same topic as one we were writing. Needless to say we rushed ours into print—the long hours were well-worth the edge we gained in the marketplace.

A shopper in Westchester, California, overheard a conversation in an elevator at the design center. One person mentioned that a certain fabric was fading and shredding in the sun. The shopper had recently worked with a local designer and happened to know that he planned to order hundreds of yards of that same material. He called his client, told him what he had learned, and saved the decorator thousands of dollars. This kind of service may be beyond the contracted level, but it evidences the "bonding" that can occur between the shopping service owners and their clients.

- Buy your competitor's products. Once you have them, really look them over with care.

  - How do they work?
  - How do they hold up?
  - What makes them eye-catching?
  - What can they do?
  - What can't they do?

You can learn a great deal about what works, how it works, what to do and what not to do. According to Sheila Eby, a New York based free-lancer, one manufacturer took a competitor's "silk screened mirror" apart to see how it had been done, and found that it wasn't silk screened at all. It had just had a print put behind the glass and the glass had been sprayed with reflective coating. This one shopping expedition saved the manufacturer thousands of dollars and reduced a seven-step manufacturing process to three steps.

- Read your trade journals and local newspapers, or hire a clipping service to search and clip relevant articles for you. It is amazing how much can be gleaned from brief articles. You may also want to make use of some computerized information services, or order magazine tear sheets for given articles identified by a quick micro fiche search by topic.

- Purchase your competitor's stock—you will get a prospectus and annual reports.

- Look for new product announcements, sales data, profit and loss statements, even patent applications, DBA's or business announcements in local legal journals. All of this information is in the public domain and can be readily secured by those who know their way around the data sources.

MYSTERY SHOPPING

The success edge literally goes to those who take the initiative—that can be you!

It is only fair to admit that not everyone is as enthusiastic about mystery shopping and monitoring as we are. There are those who see the positives of such a program and those who focus on the negatives. Let's look at both sides.

Positive View	**Negative View**
It improves management.	It invades privacy.
It assures quality service.	It reduces productivity.
It increases productivity.	It leads to more stress.

Who is right? There is no doubt that it does improve the possibility of good management. The information needed for an implementation plan for results is available. The outcome of given behaviors is obvious and can be used as a base for communication and training which might otherwise not be possible because the information might not be available.

When we know what is needed, it is often far easier to provide it correctly the first time than it is to redo it later. When this is understood and the skills/knowledge base is in place, it would be more likely to assume that productivity and quality would improve.

Other monitoring processes have been introduced, too. Most telephone companies measure how quickly operators handle customer reports, and calls exceeding a certain period of minutes are reported and action taken. Similar timing approaches are used in various airline reservation centers and for workers in various government and private agencies. The fact that this monitoring is often unknown to the person being monitored has led to some serious efforts by the Communications Workers of America to prohibit it.

Those companies that use the monitoring system just named note that the practice is a valuable management tool when it is used properly. One large firm was interested in improving its telephone contracts. Training classes were held for the employees. They were told that monitoring would take place, and that the first tape would be given to those monitored for their review and action. The second tape—which would not be made until several weeks after the first had been returned to them—would be given to them and their "partner" for review, discussion, and action. After several weeks, another tape would be made. This time the person taped, the partner, and the consultant would sit down and discuss what had been recorded and identify any changes still needed. It was this third report—and this report only—that would be shared with the supervisor. From it, goals would be developed as the baseline for part of the evaluation process.

This step-by-step process gives those involved ample time to bring about needed changes. Thus, making it possible for the final taping to be a positive presentation of their telephone skills and manner.

Recently pressures have mounted to legislate a change in the process—if lawmakers have their way—a beep will sound when monitoring occurs. Those opposing the proposed legislation contend that when a person is so alerted the conversation heard is not a natural one and will not provide a valid picture of what occurs at other times.

WHAT CAN MYSTERY SHOPPERS DO FOR YOU?

- Assess all areas (from courtesy to salesmanship) through fact-to-face encounters.
- Assess telephone techniques through call-ins.
- Investigate your competition's current business trends and sales presentations.
- Monitor your representatives who are promoting your latest idea, product, or strategy.
- Monitor franchisees for franchise compliance.

- Increase employee performance and morale by awarding on the spot prizes for meeting standards. *

- Design customized comment cards and tabulation systems for at-a-glance results.

- Conduct on-site customer surveys.

- Provide a computerized results package.

- Customize training programs and seminars.

* Standards can range from established sales quotas, not items (maybe something that isn't selling) for which sales goals are set, cleanliness and work site appearance, a minimal sales level, or interdepartmental competition.

DON'T FORGET THE CUSTOMER

Nordstrom claims that a 36% sales gain in one year was due to two things: a realization that existing customers are their most valuable asset, and an awareness that the people who serve the existing customers are their most valuable players. Their motto is, "Coddle the customers," and they do! See Appendix for the complete version.

> **"Customer relations should be a reflection of customer concerns."**
>
> **Harold Jackson**
> **J. D. N. Enterprises**

Airlines are becoming very aware of the importance of knowing more about the reactions of passengers. All but two of the airlines, Delta and Northwest, have instituted some kind of a surveillance program, and even those two have a reporting system. It happens to be run by frequent traveling executives. More and more emphasis is being placed upon the customer and his/her reactions. A study done by the U. S. Department of Transportation identified major irritants for flyers—now it will be up to the industry to monitor and change.

This attitude may be growing in importance in the marketplace, but one quick look at management textbooks will tell you that it is given little priority there. That doesn't mean it is one bit less important! So it is up to you to take action once your monitoring system has been activated. Remember, "the personal touch is becoming increasingly significant...in a world that grows more complex every day," and meeting customers needs to become a habit too entrenched to break.

9

FROM THE TOP DOWN

"Most people who start a new career have good intentions. They want to work hard and do a good job. If we are supportive of their efforts, accessible to respond to their ideas for improvements, and get out of their way, there is no limit to what they can accomplish."

James F. Nordstrom
Co-Chairman
Nordstrom, Inc.

Management really can make it happen. They set the tone and direction of a company. That sounds trite, but it's true. What's at the top is what's at the bottom.. Take a well-oiled, well-managed department and let the manager leave. For a while all will run smoothly, but eventually it will slow down like an antique phonograph, and conversely, the best ideas even die or fade away if there is no commitment at the "top." The energy of the leader's belief, the power of the dream shared is enough to put life into an organization, its plan, and its projects.

FROM THE TOP DOWN

Employees for the most part want to perform well, serve well, and get good feedback for a job well done. When they don't, the real fault usually lies elsewhere—they aren't getting the support needed, have too little information, or the basic organizational structure is inhibiting. Management creates the conditions and must monitor and change as needed to make certain that the quality of excellence is possible and the efforts rewarded.

Set the goals high, model the system, and stay in touch. The CEO is really the strongest or weakest link in the program. When top management **believes, acts, models, monitors, supports,** and **rewards,** employees emulate and red ink turns black. The management team must "walk what it talks," and know what it means.

> **"Healthy conflict and constructive critiques do more than improve our operation—they enable us to objectively see each other's strengths and weaknesses. We, as a group, grow closer and stronger."**
>
> **Dustan Goodell**
> **Resident Manager**
> **The Worthington**

Companies like The Worthington run on the principle that the key to success lies in quality and customer service.

> **"Every employee must serve the customer directly—or damn well be working hard to serve a fellow employee who is."**
>
> **Jeff Trigger**
> **General Manager**
> **The ADOLPHUS**

The time has passed when an "ivory tower" manager should be applauded. If management isn't out there meeting staff, listening to comments, praising achievements, and noting concerns, then it is giving a very clear message to staff, and the staff will model their behavior after what they see. After all, would management model what was inappropriate behavior? You bet it would and does! Like the parent who runs a stop sign but can't understand why Johnny ignores rules, most of those managers give lip service to customer service, service with a smile, but don't demonstrate it. "Actions do speak louder than words."

Those managers who care demonstrate that they

- respect people's time
- encourage them to share ideas
- keep meetings short and on track
- collect information informally
- meet with, and are interested in, their staff
- are visible and serve as facilitators
- seek constant improvement

The importance of middle management can't be ignored, but with that recognition must also come the realization that so-called middle management is having problems. Many haven't the slightest idea what is really expected of them. Years ago, one of the authors came back from a vacation to find that she had been promoted into middle management. She was surprised, went into the vice-president's office and asked what her duties would be. His answer was classic, "Well, we aren't sure. We know we need this position, but we didn't decide what it should involve. So for now just do what you think is needed, but don't make anyone mad." Now that is a directive guaranteed to stop all action, and it did for several days. It wasn't until she decided that inaction was more annoying to her and others than action, that she stepped out and "created" a job to go with the title.

The next promotion clearly illustrated another problem facing mid-level management—lack of training. Her next move was to corporate headquarters where she was asked if she have ever managed a budget. She said no, not really. The response was, "Oh, can you handle you checkbook?" "Of course." "Good, then you will have no trouble with this."

She has a wealth of information in her field, knew how to orchestrate people, was a great facilitator, but when the budget printout arrived on her desk, it threw her into a tailspin—it looked like pages and pages of Greek. No one had told her what was to be done, or how it was to be managed. She had heard about creative budgeting, but this was insane—she either had to get trained or "create" a whole new system. She got the training, but some of her peers tried to struggle through the quagmire alone with predictable results. All of them would have been far more productive and far more comfortable had some time been taken to give them guidelines and/or training.

These may be amusing incidents in one person's life, but unfortunately, similar experiences can be cited by most managers. Jobs that are poorly defined and training that is weak or missing is noted as a problem by many managers.

> **"Experience [and training are] what enable you to recognize a mistake when you make it."**
>
> **Earl Wilson**

Luckily, most managers, or, at least many, do get the technical training needed, but few have the background or training that is needed for the emotional and behavioral management they must do. They need specific information and even more important, they need good, preferably outstanding, role models. Top management needs to lead by example and let them know what is expected of them.

The best way this can happen is to develop a strong team. A good team is one that taps talents, fosters communication, stresses the value of the individual and his/her ideas, and has the support of upper management By making certain that the team represents the six behavioral styles. You build strength because

- **Leaders** provide direction
- **Persuaders** sell ideas and provide enthusiasm
- **Patient People** stress an analytical approach
- **Careful People** check details and keep things on target
- **Reserved People** insist on logic and sequence
- **Independent People** are willing to break out of their comfort zone and tackle the unknown.

Together they can find answers far more readily than can one person.

Stressing team work, valuing people, and communication isn't enough. If you want to ensure success, you also have to assess your staff. Which ones will make a commitment and which ones willingly adopt the dream of a service-driven company or organization. Those that won't or can't may fit in well elsewhere, but they have no place in a company with this focus. Take those who do fit and **show** them what you mean and what you want. Get the message to the people, get out of your own comfort zone and **make** it happen. Start with managers, put the message across, and they, in turn, can take it to the rest of the staff. Memos don't make an impact, guidelines don't bring change, but your example can do both.

EVALUATING THE STAFF OF A SERVICE-DRIVEN BUSINESS

When you move into this operational mode, you need to make a commitment to it from the onset. Your performance system needs to have service performance measurement incorporated, and an incentive program that indicates your commitment will emphasize your interest in quality service and customer satisfaction.

Management sets the tone and the evaluation needs to involve five areas:

- A knowledge of what you really want—clear goals and expectations. Each job is different, and only the persons in that position really know what they can do to benefit the customers. Ask each to identify specific goals targeting customer satisfaction. The shipping clerk might set the goal of "deliveries properly addressed, packaged, and shipped within 'x' time of request."

- After they decide what they should do, ask them to outline how they will insure that it is done, and provide some quantifiable measures to show that it has occurred.

- Determine base measurements. There are many that can be used. We mentioned sales—number, dollars, but you could also track the number of customer complaints, the number of compliments received in writing per week or month, the number of appointments booked and kept. You will be able to identify the right measurement base if you will just give it some thought.

- Give feedback. There are many ways, but the process is not the important factor, the feedback is.

- Reward extra effort, and those rewards should be part of an individualized incentive program.
  - Some people are profit-oriented and want a *piece of the action.*
  - Another might want *time off*
  - Some want to be *promoted.*
  - Still others want *recognition in front of their peers.*
  - There are those who seek *freedom from the*

clock or a chance for *personal growth* (i.e., paid tuition).

When all of this is in place, each employee can say, and know that it is true, that he or she will be rewarded in direct proportion to his own production. Remember when you were in school, and some student asked what grade the teacher had "given" him/her? Well, like the wise teacher, you should be able to tell each employee, "I don't give grades. I tabulate performance." Each staff member should realize that real power lies within themselves. Others can encourage and train us, but only we can control what we become.

Leadership success demands that you

- Tap into the power of communication.
- Change those things that you can change.
- Deal with those that you can't change.
- **Learn** to know the difference.

Control over people is not the answer to success but consistency, caring, and credibility are the real issues.

Enthusiasm coupled with energy makes one of the best role models you can provide. If a picture is worth a thousand words than an example must be worth a thousand orders.

TEACH YOUR STAFF TO MIRROR THE WINNERS

Help them avoid the pitfalls that lead to failure.Those who fail

- are self-focused
- don't risk
- see parts of the picture
- are happy with what they know
- live in their own world
- see the negatives
- lack a sense of humor
- focus on rote work
- aren't flexible
- give up easily
- shirk responsibility
- have limited influence
- lack forgiveness
- often hate their work

Encourage them to emulate the successful who

- are sensitive to others
- leave their "comfort zone"
- see the big picture
- keep learning

- are involved in the world
- see the positives
- have a sense of humor
- are creative
- learn from change
- bounce back
- assume responsibility
- are influential
- are forgiving
- and enjoy their work.

CUSTOMERS DESERVE THE BEST

10

INVEST IN YOUR STAFF: SELECTION AND TRAINING

"Don't confuse effort with results. Don't confuse efficiency with effectiveness."

James Jacobson
Chairman Emeritus
Beneficial Standard Life Insurance Company

Companies in the U.S.A. spend in excess of $30 billion a year on corporate training—a figure that is impressive until you compare it with the corporate hardware bill of $400 billion. As Tom Peters said in an article appearing in the *San Diego Union,* "Our training spending, only 75 cents per employee per day, is a pale shadow of the training commitment of our most fearsome competitors such as West Germany and Japan."

Ask any manager, and most employees, and they will tell you that the most expensive asset of most businesses is the staff. Yet, all too often these same managers and executives will willingly invest millions in hardware maintenance and little, or none in designing effective hiring, screening, and placement procedures or in human development and maintenance. It is not unusual to hear statements like these:

- It is difficult to find competent help in this areas.
- We hire only those with experience or training.
- We had to make some budget cuts, so we cut out the frills and reduced our human resources budget.

These same individuals will willingly authorize

- the purchase of personal computers and then let them sit underutilized—or unused—because they won't invest in staff training.

> **"Technology is an important management tool—but don't let it get in the way of the guest's experience."**
>
> **Bill Hulett**
> **CEO**
> **Stouffer Hotels**

- the expansion of phone systems and then fail to train their staff to use them effectively and efficiently.

- a contract with a head-hunter but to not predefine the behaviors that are needed to perform a given job.

- the rehabilitation of corporate offices to improve image and impact, and then fail to provide staff with the tools and knowledge needed to ensure that the "people facet of the image" is the best that it can be.

In other words, they miss the point—only with effective training, and on-going support, can a staff know what needs to be done, and know how to get it done so that it meets both the needs of the company and customer.

To make certain that there is no gap between your mission and your execution, you need to have a staff that makes it happen. Getting that staff and training it is your responsibility if you are the manager. The buck really does stop at management.

THE RIGHT CHOICE MAKES A DIFFERENCE

No one takes a job thinking, "Oh, boy, another chance to fail," and no one seeks staff thinking, "Oh, great, now I can really fix this one." Employers want and need competent employees, and employees seek and want jobs that let them use their talents to the fullest. What goes wrong? There is a void in the hiring process.

Many companies decide what they want in a job by looking at the duties and considering

- the departmental needs—typing, filing, answering phones, etc.
- the pay level they can afford to offer.
- the benefit package that goes with it.
- the level (secretarial, clerk, mid-level management) of the position.
- the years of experience that would be desirable.
- the type of education that is needed.

Next, an ad is placed and applications begin to arrive. They are asked to prove with resumés and recommendations (many of which are now of limited value since employers must be very careful about "defamation" of character) what they indicate to be true on the application. An interview is held, and personal impact is considered. The next step—decide. Oh yes, there may have been a skills test in there somewhere, or in some companies, simulations of actual situations. What's wrong with the process? A great deal!

WHY DON'T WE KEEP EMPLOYEES?

Let's look at why people are dismissed. We let staff go when

- they can't get along with others
- they are too involved (too many personal calls) interfering with others' productive time
- they assume too little responsibility
- they assume too much authority
- their production is too limited
- there are personality conflicts
- they take on too much and then don't do it well
- they don't follow rules or regulations
- they are slaves to rules and regulations and will not bend
- they are too perfectionistic and overdo everything
- they are careless and make too many errors.

None of these behaviors would appear in the hiring process unless the last employer mentioned them. Also, in some instances what is a negative in one position may well be a positive in another. What is needed is a means of assessing behaviors (i.e., an instrument like **JOB CHECK**) that can be used before an employee is sought. Instruments such as this identify the pace, authority, interactive, and rule compliance levels needed to successfully perform in the position. Then, the applicant's own behavioral pattern can be assessed via instruments such as **QUICK CHECK** and through recommendations as part of the overall screening. When the skills needed are present, the educational base is there, the experience is sufficient, and the behaviors match—you have the right employee!

To determine needs, ask yourself these questions:

- Do I want someone who
  - can assume a directive mode and manage a number of people?
  - will be responsible for his/her desk and related tasks only?
  - takes direction from others and makes no decisions on his/her own?

- Does the position require
  - a person who is enthusiastic, outgoing, and gregarious?
  - an individual who is pleasant to others, but doesn't waste time interacting?

- someone who can work alone and deal with ideas and concepts independently of others?

- Does this job demand

  - that all tasks be thoroughly and analytically approached—one task at a time with closure being secured before another task is undertaken?
  - that a moderately fast pace is used—four or five tasks under way at the same time?
  - that myriad tasks can be handled simultaneously without losing control over them or oneself?

- Will the person in this position have to

  - be perfectionistic and concerned about rules and regulations?
  - maintain a good level of accuracy but not be overly involved with rules?
  - take risks, be innovative, take on assignments for which there are no guidelines or precedents?

Before you can expect someone to do the job to your satisfaction, you must first know what would give you satisfaction. We seldom fire people for what they know or don't know—we checked that out before they came to work, but we do become very irritated when their behaviors don't match our expectations—even if we never identified those expectations. Mind reading is not yet an exact science, although many of us expect it in our employees.

After we know what we want in the way of behaviors, we can ask the present employee and the prospective employee what he or she believes the job entails in the four areas noted above. Be aware that a discrepancy means that the two parties—you and the employee—need to sit down, discuss, and perhaps even redefine the job.

Selecting the right staff is no accident, it takes planning. However, there are ten important points that need to be considered.

POINT ONE

- You certainly want the best person for the job and the most qualified. But to serve your wide customer base you would offer employment opportunities to all. Remember, customers come in all sizes, races, and creeds—and you should offer employment opportunities to the same diverse base. This is the law of the land, and the unwritten law of the marketplace.

POINT TWO

- Ask your customers—find out what kind of results they want when

    - they call in for information
    - they need a service call
    - they place an order
    - they enter the store or office
    - or they check on a bill.

- Factor their responses into your job analysis.

POINT THREE

- Consider motivators, they are based upon our values system. Values need to blend but there are also times when you do not want a clone but a complement. You may find yourself drawn to particular candidates because they remind you (unconsciously) of yourself. If you hire such a person, there may be two of you who can't do what you need done.

- In other words, evaluate what needs to be done that the present staff can't do effectively—hire to fill those voids. This means that there will be times when job descriptions need to be revamped.

POINT FOUR

- Know your own "hot buttons" and make certain that your candidate is alerted (and staff is informed). If you are a "bear on timeliness" it won't do for an employee to be late even if all the work gets done. The person may think that that is unfair and it may be, but if it bothers you, it will eventually become an issue of major proportions.

POINT FIVE

- Give the real message—tailor the job flyers to pre-screen out those who would not fit. (See the chart at the end of this section).

POINT SIX

- Build your application to provide additional behavioral information. You can word the questions in such a way that you will know pace pattern, interactive needs, level of leadership, and the extent to which the person is rule-conscious or rule-directed.

- For example, if you have a question on your application dealing with outside activities, go on and find out how many positions of power the person has held and for how long. What was involved in those positions? You will then know if the individual is comfortable with authority and willing to provide direction to others.

- A question on outside interests and hobbies will provide you with information on interaction. The person who spends all of his/her time reading, writing, or painting is probably not going to be the most gregarious person in the company. Just to be sure, have a follow-up section to the questions which finds out more than the "when, how, and with whom."

POINT SEVEN

- Use open-ended interview questions. The person will tell you a great deal more about him/herself if you don't design questions that limit answers to one word or a single phrase.

POINT EIGHT

- You want people who are goal-directed, self-motivated and willing to go "that extra mile." Set up some scenarios and ask what the person would do if that happened. The answers will be invaluable.

POINT NINE

- Make certain that you use panels or multiple interviewers. Cliches don't exist without reason—they are truisms, and none more true than "Two heads are better than one." Just as you want two doctors' opinions before surgery, you should have several opinions before you entrust your reputation to an employee.

POINT TEN

- Build on your strengths. Wouldn't it be great if you could clone your best employees? Well, there is no reason why you can't take a major step in that direction—use success profiles based upon tools such as **QUICK CHECK.** By determining the behavioral patterns of the employees most successful and effective in given positions, by identifying the communalities of those patterns, you can compare those to the job behavioral needs and come up with hiring guidelines—and later training guidelines—that will help you literally "clone" your best staff members.

ONCE THEY'RE HIRED, THEN WHAT?

Management often gives a strong message to staff, "Meet the needs of the clients and customers, keep productivity and profits, up, and beat out the competition." This is a message worth remembering, but if the staff doesn't know what to do to accomplish those objectives, they will

- try but fail
- try and accidently succeed
- be scared to try for fear they will do it wrong
- try and fall short of the best they could do with training.

WHY IS TECHNICAL TRAINING IMPORTANT?

- to make certain that equipment is operated properly.
- to insure that productivity is fostered and increased by avoiding down-time (employee and machinery).

WHY IS PERFORMANCE TRAINING IMPORTANT?

- to make certain that customer problems are anticipated and solved.
- to make certain that angry, irate customers are satisfied and return to use the products and services again.
- to make certain that each staff member has the skills needed to "operate" effectively.
- to build self-esteem and let staff know you care about and believe in them—people rise to your level of expectation.
- to insure that the business **grows** and **prospers.**
- to show the staff how to build sound relationships based upon trust and confidence.
- to provide staff with the skills needed to turn a difficult, angry customer into a satisfied one.
- to give each individual a sound basis of self-understanding and the ability to "read" and relate appropriately to others—customers and colleagues.
- to show each person how to take the negative and turn it into a positive that builds both good will and business.
- to make it possible for each person to mirror and relate—the keys to the vital bonding that makes people return again and again.

Once your staff has mastered these techniques, you

have the assurance that they can do what you have wanted to happen all along—do things right the first time, satisfy the customer, and enhance the image of the company or organization.

WHAT IS GOOD TRAINING?

Good training is a well-paced progression toward a worthwhile goal—in this case, profit, productivity, and good customer service. It needs to be

- fun
- supported by upper management
- on-going (no one-shot, band-aid approaches)
- custom-tailored to your company (pre-packaged programs rarely meet everyone's requirements).

Once you decide to institute training, you need to make certain that

- you do a Needs Analysis to identify your resources.
- develop, or have a consultant develop, an on-going program in which the materials are broken down into manageable increments that permit mastery of the parts.
- the program provides each employee with the skills needed to empower him/her to achieve the

positive results wanted.
- your staff is involved and know what **benefits** are in this for **them**.

Set forth below are some of the questions we ask when clients ask us to prepare a Needs Assessment for them.

- Who will be attending the sessions?
- Will top management be trained with the others or first? (Note: program success is often a trickle-down process—if support staff knows that upper management has a commitment to the process, so will they).
- What are the major issues or problems faced by your industry, your company, the department or group to be trained?
- What prior training has the group had before? By whom? When?
- How is this program expected to fit in with the company goals or objectives?
- What are the strengths of the group to be trained?
- What, if any, are the weaknesses? Which of those should be addressed by this program?
- You should be aware of any specific problems faced by this group.

Are you going to use an outside agency or consultant to provide the program? You may want to suggest to them that they use your answers as they plan. In addition, we have found it very helpful to talk to key people by phone, conduct personal interviews (in-person when possible), secure information via news-letters, trade journals, annual reports, etc. All of this information provides us with a base of commonality within those in the program. The importance of this was brought home to us last year when we prepared and presented a program for a waste disposal company headquartered in San Francisco. During the program, we made reference to examples related to the industry and how what we were presenting could help effective communication with clients or others. At the end of the program, an older manager came up and said, "I know I needed presentation skills, but I was very doubtful if an **outsider** could help me be effective in my field. Your early references to our company and industry and your ability to show us practical uses and approaches related to our industry convinced me to listen and try out your idea." Obviously, we are not waste disposal specialists, but research had given us a common ground from which to work.

REINFORCEMENT LOCKS IN LEARNING

Studies and practical experience have convinced us that the successful programs should incorporate:

- familiar material and build on past learnings and experience.
- hands-on activities
- role playing
- a three-part pattern: initial training, practice time, and follow-up sessions to reinforce and augment earlier input.
- recognition of successful participation (accreditation programs, certificates, salary increments).
- demonstration of mastery through an assessment and on-job performance check.
- opportunities to practice the skills learned.

In addition, it is essential that the changes be integral to the workings of the entire department, division, and/or company. True, when one person changes the dance step, the dance must change, but to be truly effective, the music and dance should go together (i.e., the workplace must be able to support and encourage the needed changes.) If we ask employees to become front line decision makers, we will need to support their decisions and provide them with the resources that make it possible.

CUSTOMER SERVICE TRAINING IS MULTIFACETED

Effective customer service training is on-going, multifaceted, and part of the very fiber of a company; it is not limited to one approach. When we problem solve with clients, they initially focus on formal classroom programs conducted by professionals. Let's start right there. If that is what you plan to do, and nothing more, **skip it**! Training should be an integral part of the ongoing activities within your organization, and it needs to encompass

- classroom programs
- matched mentors (each staff member should be matched to mentors who can answer questions, make suggestions, or demonstrate effective approaches.)
- OJT (On-the-Job Training)
- opportunities to problem solve and implement new strategies
- opportunities to view, analyze, and evaluate competitors, and then make suggestions for appropriate innovations.

Each of these activities needs to be designed to insure that the best service is given while providing the best learning environment and support.

ON-THE-JOB-TRAINING

On-the-job training is too important to ignore. Recently, we were waiting impatiently in a long check-out line at a local market. We noticed that the cashier seemed to be having difficulty with the bar-code reader. As those in line became more and more impatient, she became more and more upset and less and less efficient. Finally, the manager sensed the growing tension and came over to help her. Much to our surprise—and later admiration—she did not take over and speed through it. Instead, she provided support for the girl and for us—she kept her tone soft, her manner confident, and conveyed to us and the cashier her faith in the girl's ability. She was there to help, but not to mother, and her support eased the tension. The cashier's anxiety level dropped and she was able to remember what needed to be done and how to do it. True, it might have been faster for us if the manager had taken over completely—but by conducting a quick on-the-job training session, the manager increased her employee's self-confidence. The cashier was able to serve us well, and will go on to serve others efficiently in the future.

SELF-DIRECTED LEARNING

Self-directed learning can build self-confidence. Those who lack self-confidence often are so fearful of failure that it interferes with their successful completion of tasks. They over-prepare, cling to rules, hesitate to act, and hide behind regulations or only act when sure that they can win. You and your company are the real losers because they don't share ideas, don't act in a timely manner and may miss opportunities that should have been capitalized upon.

> **"Happy people are more productive and may well have an edge when they apply for jobs or when they are considered for promotions."**
>
> **William Verwolf**
> **General Manager**
> **Union Camp**

Part of the training focus should be devoted to building self-esteem and self-confidence. Consider the self-esteem circle—each section represents an area in which we can have self-confidence.

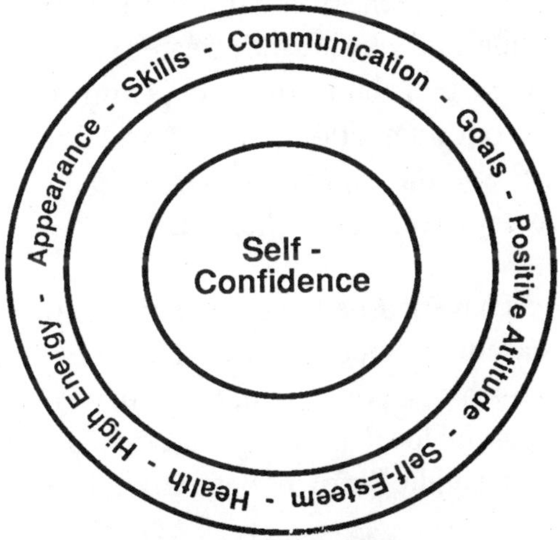

INVEST IN YOUR STAFF

When we have self-confidence in several areas, we develop a good self-esteem which then makes it possible for us to risk.

A well-designed training program can help each person maximize his or her potential.

Area of Self-Confidence	**Ways to Foster Self-Confidence**
Appearance	Tips on dress and grooming
Skills	Formal, on-job training
Communication	Coaching, training, opportunities
Goals	Reward goal-setting
Positive attitude	Techniques for developing
Self-Esteem	Mentors, feedback and recognition
Health	Training/balanced menus in cafeteria
High energy	Stress reduction/exercise programs

It is said that "all men are equal." If true, why do some feel less equal and why are they treated as if they were? Often how we feel about ourselves is mirrored back to us through our interaction with others. You owe it to employees and the organization to help each person feel good about himself or herself.

Executives have learned that a change in appearance can increase their success ratio. Give your staff the same edge—hire a consultant, bring in a color representative, invite local stores to send in image consultants, and provide "brown bag university" classes (lunchtime programs). We are more comfortable when we are with those most like us—this goes for your clients and customers as well. In addition, your employees will be more effective when they know they look their best. Help them meet this goal.

Each of us needs three mentor groups:

- two people from our own field—a man and a woman—in order to learn from the best and gain the perspectives they have.
- members of our professional organizations. Learn from those who have been there and use your own energy to move ahead instead of reinventing the wheel.
- your own personal "Pity party—Brag group". "Pity party" friends understand that there are times when we strike out and need to tell someone who knows that that doesn't make us losers. "Brag group" friends listen appreciatively as we list our accomplishments without thinking we are being obnoxious braggarts.

Encourage your staff to secure these groups, and help them if help is needed.

ORGANIZING THE TRAINING

There are some guidelines that need to be followed in order to insure that training programs are as effective as possible.

- Select the right instructors.
  - If they are in-house instructors they should
    - have the ability to make effective presentations
    - have the confidence of the staff.
  - If they are outside consultants they should
    - have knowledge of the industry
    - know the inner workings or your company.
  - In addition, for outside consultants, you should investigate the consultant's credentials, client list, and ask for a written proposal which
    - notes topic and background information
    - indicates proposed approach and agenda

- notes that the program will be custom tailored to your company. Beware of generic outlines.
- states timelines, time frames, and costs for
    - program design
    - presentation
    - workbook design.
- states that the workbook will belong to you, excluding any copyrighted materials, for internal use as you see fit.
- indicates how follow-up should be handled.

Do not base your decision solely on price. A consultant who has a seemingly high fee may be willing to train the trainers or provide you with a workbook that makes it possible to replicate the program. This would be a good investment—far better than a program that came cheap but could not be replicated.

BUT THERE'S NO BUDGET!

Don't give the weakest excuse of all—there's no money! We make choices, and we choose which programs and expenditures are to be given priority and which will be cut or eliminated. Let's take the worst scenarios—there truly is **no** money! Nonsense, that merely means that there is no money in your budget. There are other sources, and if effective service is your goal, take the time to secure that money and find those funding sources.

Grants: Companies like Kodak and Collins Foods have full time staff members who do nothing but seek funding sources. Other companies work closely with such organizations as the National Funded Training Council in California. This council helps its members find funding and service sources, even writing the grants and proposals for them.

Local Educational Institutions: Tap into your local colleges and universities, both public and private. There are many ways to do so, and your staff can do the legwork or utilize the services of groups like the council named above to find, arrange, and orchestrate the training.

Special service organizations: Investigate services such as SCORE (Service Corp of Retired Executives), RSVP (Retired Seniors Volunteer Program), and JTP (Job Training Program).

Consultants: Consider hiring a consultant team to take a look at your needs. They will work with you in a focused problem solving session to design a training program that can be presented to your entire staff, or just to your designated trainers who can then replicate it without additional cost.

Reduce hidden costs: Look at turnover, absenteeism, and employee dissatisfaction, and calculate the costs. Determine the causes via a focused problem solving session. Work out programs or systems that will minimize those problems. Effective training will reduce or eliminate these hidden costs.

Once the person is on board, you and your staff have a responsibility to

- provide the technical training needed to perform the job correctly.
- note the company's mission and position statement as it relates to customer service.
- provide a contact who can answer questions and serve as a mentor.
- note the company's position on teamwork and quality circles.
- provide the interpersonal, communication, and management training needed.

INVEST IN YOUR STAFF

Remember that the companies that are industry's pace setters make good customer service a priority in their training programs. If you don't provide the training needed, your staff will work out systems and methods that help them cope in the most efficient way they know. Their approaches may or may not fit in with your goals and expectations. If they do, you are lucky. If they don't, you're responsible.

KEY WORDS AND JOB MATCHING

STYLE	APPROACH	KEY WORDS	JOB MATCHES
Leader	Pragmatic	Direct Results-based Ambitious Energetic Assured	Manager Administrator Buyer Salesperson Politician
Persuader	Sensory	Warm Sociable Impulsive Easily hurt Results-based	Salesperson Human Resource The Arts Politician Promoter
Patient	Analytical	Thorough Warm Traditional Polite Process-based	Lawyer Teaching Counselor Social Work Psychologist
Careful	Precise	Cautious Diplomatic Perfectionist Cooperative	Programmer Actuary Surgeon Missionary
Reserved	Logical	Analytical Process-based Aloof/shy Conceptual Rational	Engineer Inventor Chemist Analyst Biologist
Independent	Innovative	Direct Results-based Adventurous Energetic Imaginative	Entrepreneur Manager Explorer Builder Developer

11

TEAMWORK: THE HIDDEN ASSET

"Inspire your team. Most industrial managers... have paid more attention to the development of the machine than they ever gave to the development of man. The oncoming industrialist...must develop man first."

James F. Lincoln
from his book *Incentive Management*

The potential for excellence is in us all, and when that potential is multiplied by tapping the talents of a diverse group of people—all working for the same goal and all following the same service-driven guidelines—there is no doubt about the outcome.

In order to be an effective team, there are certain precepts that must be followed:

- the team must have the support of management
- there must be a commitment to institute

changes that are plausible, fiscally sound, and feasible.
- the team must be balanced for talents and behaviors.

- when problems are considered, the problem solving session should be designed so that there is

  - a **Leader** who can provide direction.
  - a **Persuader** who will be able to convey the plans to others in ways that will make them "buy" into them.
  - a **Patient Person** who will provide the analytical, thorough approach so necessary to a successful team.
  - a **Careful Person** who will keep everyone on track and make certain that guidelines and regulations are followed.
  - A **Reserved Person** who will provide the logical, sequential approach needed—if efforts are made to involve the person who tends not to volunteer action or information, but often has great ideas.
  - an **Independent Person** who will provide the "it may never have been done before, but let's try it attitude" that is all too often lacking in those who tend to stay in their comfort zone.

- and there must be a chairperson who understands each of the styles and is able to work with all of them—appropriately motivating each to reach his/her full potential.

INVOLVE EVERYONE

Once the base plans have been made by the team, there is a need to make certain that all of those involved—directly or indirectly—are told what is expected, the results sought, and asked for their suggestions and help. Plans work best when the ideas and plans are "owned" by everyone.

In some instances, there will be a need to educate those involved not merely in their job but also in how to interface with other "customers" (colleagues). How do the jobs interlock? We work more smoothly and waste less time when we know the "how" and "why" of the process.

PLAN YOUR STRATEGY

Use a strategy planning session to plan sequence, process, and interaction flow. For example, if the communication system is ineffective, put together a broad-based team (representatives from various departments, someone who interfaces directly with customers or clients—internal and external. They will be able to bring to a session information and input about the pluses of the present system as well as its problems.

REMEMBER THE ENVIRONMENT

Staff functions most effectively in an environment that is conducive to production—clean, well-organized, harmonious, comfortable, quiet, well-lit, and supportive. The responsibility for seeing that this environment is in place initially is management's, but the responsibility for keeping it in place is both management's and staff's.

MANAGERS SHOULD MINGLE

The old "open door policy" creates some major problems. Management is often put in the untenable position of hearing "gossip and being expected to act on it." The closed door policy that often follows the misuse of an open door one, may well result in distancing and a breakdown of teamwork. Both extremes need to be guarded against.

GIVE YOUR TEAM A MISSION

Team spirit doesn't just happen; it is part of a plan. The dictator can't capture employee loyalty—obedience maybe, but never loyalty. However, the employer who provides a coherent, well-developed, clearly spelled out plan coupled with a consistent foundation of trust, respect, enthusiasm, and communication will.

LEAD BY EXAMPLE

The leader and the team are a unit—and the leader must lead by example. Just as it didn't impress us as children to hear an adult say, "Don't do as I do, do as I say," it doesn't impress our staff when we say they must live by one set of values, guidelines, or rules while we govern our actions by another. If managers don't "buy into" the system, they give a loud, clear message to staff—this is a system in which we don't believe and do not value.

Effective management of a team demands that the person understand process, work effectively within structure, run on a system, and deal with role, not people. However, the next dimension—leadership—demands even more. The leader needs to deal with ideas, people, emotions, and direct communication. When the team is led by such a person, thinking is promoted, self-examination is fostered, innovation is stimulated, and analysis and logical thinking is reinforced. It is not enough to manage a team, the leader must be concerned with the substance of the procedure—what is decided and how it is communicated.

Don't misunderstand. This person will have to tell it like it is; will need to "read" the team; will need to foster change; and will have to seek results. Their excitement will be contagious, for they realize that their success depends upon

- showing others how to be successful and clearing away roadblocks and obstacles for them.
- earning respect.
- avoiding directives when they are meaningless and can't be followed.
- recognizing cause and effect relationships—the outcome of certain acts and the impact of certain statements.
- providing the support needed to get the job done.
- earning respect and accepting the fact that it may not be coupled with affection.
- being able to read the "real" message.
- delivering what is promised.

When all of this is in place, one can "tap the potential of the staff"—it takes more than one person to run a company. Everyone is not equally able to perform in every task, so don't ignore this advice

> **"Don't ever let the little fellas load the truck while all the big ones drive them."**
>
> **Maurice Kuper**
> **Executive Vice President**
> **Kimball International**

REWARDS AND INCENTIVES

Achievement needs to be recognized and rewarded appropriately—inappropriate rewards and incentives have little lasting impact other than alienation. As the team leader—call it corporate executive—considers this, he or she should also realize that the most successful motivation programs are those that are geared to help employees become achievers.

Don Burrell of Burrell Colour—in a letter to his staff—makes this point better than we can.

> [Our] program was instituted to show our appreciation to those employees who are on the job daily. We realize the efforts put forth by each of you; the loyalty shown to Burrell Colour and our customers, and the respect to your supervisor and co-workers by being here, on time, every day. This [attendance award

coupon worth $20.00] is an additional way for Burrell Colour to say, "Thank You" for a job well done. (See Appendix)

The most successful programs are those geared to help employees become achievers. Hold scheduled meetings and set up on-going systems that provide all employees with data and an understanding of what is expected and their role in its success.

Don't forget that you may never see "teamwork" or "team spirit" listed as a corporate asset, but it is the hidden, but most powerful, item on every profit and loss statement.

12

THE TELEPHONE: A SUCCESS TOOL

"Customer satisfaction is our only product and is achieved through understanding both the customers' and our requirements and responding with safe, quality, cost-effective, and innovative products, technology, and service."

Tony Amatangelo
Director of Operations
UCAR Emulsion Systems
Union Carbide Corporation

The modern world is truly dependent upon the telephone, but its real value is often ignored. It is a vital link with customers, clients, members, patron, and patients, and it is a link that should be maximized. Unfortunately, we forget its value in our rush. Our modern world is truly dependent upon the telephone, but its real value is often ignored.

Your customers deserve to have the "best" service available and that means the service you provide over the phone as well. When you make a call, you need to have all of your data and materials on hand. In addition, you need to "read" your customer and adjust to his or her behavioral type or group, use the right words, and mirror the listening language.

It is obvious that there are some things that you **must not do**

- never interrupt
- never work on other projects or shuffle papers—even signing checks distracts you, and others know when your attention is not really on them and their problems/s
- chew gum or eat while talking.

There are also some **musts**

- respond as if you were there
- take notes on what is being said—tell them you are
- repeat in your own words what was conveyed; this cuts down on errors
- repeat key points
- make phone appointments—avoid phone tag this way
- speak distinctly and enunciate carefully
- match pace
- mirror style
- take a **brief** time to build rapport

- use the person's name
- sound interested

You owe it to your customers to make certain that they are helped to communicate their needs, concerns, and interests effectively and that responses are prompt. In order to accomplish the first part of this

- the information needs to be skillfully gathered. The staff member needs to make certain that the 5 W's (who, what, where, when, why) and the 1 H (how) are all covered.
- the real needs/message must be identified.
- their objections or concerns need to be isolated or no solution is possible.
- they must know that the person is committed to making a decision and handling the problem.

In all four instances, feedback is one of the most powerful tools you can use. Of course, it is impossible to have a complete understanding of what another wants, needs, fears, or seeks, but if you will take time to listen (really listen to the words and the underlying message), to feedback what you think you heard, give them time to refute or support your perceptions, and then make comments so worded that there is room for agreement or disagreement, you will have taken a major step into effective customer service.

As you know, anger has three stages: disappointment, frustration, and then anger. What we are about to suggest can only be used with the first two of these phases. the truly angry person is not in a position emotionally to even hear or believe you when you indicate concern and a willingness to help.

If there is a good rapport, you will find that your feedback impact is maximized by lead-ins such as these: It seems that you; from your point of view; what I'm hearing is; you must mean; as you see it; now your point is.

If you have trouble building phone rapport, there are other lead-ins that may work. You might begin your feedback with phrases such as these: It appears that you; I'm not certain I understand what you mean, but; correct me if I'm wrong, but I think.

Be truly interested in the other person and the problem or concern, ask open-ended questions (these give the person a chance to expand whereas closed ended ones allow the person to fall back on "yes" or "no"); put what has been said into your own words and give the person feedback to insure that you processed it properly; and, of course, none of this can be accomplished unless you **make** and take **time** to listen—not pause, listen.

LISTENING LANGUAGES

We use all three listening languages (auditory, visual, and kinesthetic), but one of them seems to be dominant. In fact, it even affects what we enjoy, and may affect our buying habits, too. For example, visual people are attracted to form and color; auditory to sound; and kinesthetic to texture. All of this needs to be factored into your plans and promotions if you are to meet the needs of your customers.

Your feedback needs to mirror and match. If the person is visual, paint a picture for him/her.

> Can't you just picture how this is going to look when it is finished? I was amazed at how attractive the cover turned out to be, and once this report is bound, the cover sheets—which have such great graphics—are in place, and covered with that heavy, clear plastic, this will be one of the most attractive reports to come out of this office.

Or if the person is auditory, let them "hear" your message.

> I really mean it when I tell you that you will love hearing this report—the write-up is interesting—but the real meat will be in the presentation. He has

> some great sound to put with it, and the back-up audio adds a great deal to the message.

Your tone is very important—in fact so important that it can undo the entire situation. It is particularly important to the auditory person, but actually impacts on the other styles as well. Remember that 55% of your impact comes from your tone.

If the other person is kinesthetic, he or she needs to "feel" the message.

> Let me share something with you. This report is really going to have an impact—he has worked hard to gather data that will affect every single department head here. If you will pay close attention, you will have no difficulty grasping the enormity of this report and the significance it is going to have to all of us.

With a little practice, you can use this technique with anyone, and when you then couple it with appropriate words, a tone that indicates concern and interest, and gestures that support all of this, you will have enhanced that vital relationship with the customers.

Many customers are frustrated by the written and oral communication they encounter. In part this is because others forget, or, do not know how to **mirror**. But another reason lies in the fact that many have not learned one of the most important communication guidelines: start with your main point briefly stated; develop it with data, quotations, or references to experts; and then restate the main point and its significance to the situation or issue. This can be done orally or in writing, but it **is essential**.

It is also important that you not "buy" into another's mood or frustration when you encounter them in person or on the phone. Take a moment or two and identify the behavior being exhibited—do you really want to reinforce it?

If you are dealing with someone on your staff whose behaviors are not desirable, you can't reprogram them, but you can contribute to some major changes anyway. Reward the behavior you like and thus reinforce it, ignore or address the behavior you don't like. (i.e., If someone has been answering the phones without giving his/her name, and you observe them answering appropriately, tell them so and let them know you are pleased.)

Spot checks will help you monitor phone service and good feedback will help those you supervise know what you like and don't like and want changed. When staff is treated like a prized customer, the role model is in place that will encourage them to treat their colleagues and customers as VIPs.

BASIC TELEPHONE PROTOCOL

Every staff member needs to follow some basic protocol when using the telephone—your customers deserve it.

- **Be ready** with paper and pencil on hand and resources and manuals nearby.
- **Be knowledgeable** about company policy, regulations, services, and products.
- **Be warm** and take a minute to build rapport by asking questions, identifying behavior type. Use appropriate key words, and mirror the listening language.
- **Present information** in a multi-sensory way.
- **Tie down the conclusion** by restating what has been decided, confirming what each of you is to do, agreeing on deadlines, and establishing checkpoints if needed.
- **Thank them** and use their name—mean it!
- **Preplan** your calls by jotting down the main points to be made and put them in order of importance.
- **Get off the phone promptly.**
- **Answer calls** efficiently and effectively by picking up between ring 2 and 4 (the first ring is seldom heard by the caller).
- **Give your name and the department** (but remember, the first two words are throw-aways).

- **Don't interrupt.**
- **Get the caller's name and use it.**
- **Never promise to have a call returned**, only promise to give the message.
- **Always have phone coverage**—you, a colleague, or voice mail.

It is important to know yourself—so get a mirror and put it where you can see yourself while talking. Look in it. You will find that pleasant expressions coupled with pleasant tones lead to good relations. It is also important to enunciate clearly to reduce confusion which often leads to frustration and anger.

Remember, 93% of all contacts are made over the telephone; therefore, we need to remember how important phone contacts have become to service-driven businesses. We can't do without it, but some of us need to improve our telephone skills.

Put that phone system to work for you. It is a sophisticated marketing tool, an effective communication link with your customers, and one of your best forms of advertisement when it is used effectively.

13

TAKE CHARGE OF CHANGE

"You don't get a second chance to make a first impression. And it's the customer's perception that counts."

Howard G. Seebach
DuPont

Superior customer service demands that you stay alert and step with care through the mine fields of change—the change that your competitors are triggering. If you forget, if you get careless and don't identify these potentially explosive situations, or if you have slow reaction time, you face serious consequences.

There is a real danger in not realizing the real difference between what customers really want and what you believe they want. Look at the position of Domino's

Pizza and that of Pizza Hut. These two companies zeroed in and narrowed their markets. Pizza Hut moved from a Spartan setting to a family ambiance and provides a pleasant atmosphere for on-site eating. Domino's noted that there were many who called in orders and only stayed on-site long enough to pick them up. So, although Pizza Hut will deliver, Domino's has built a delivery system that sets the standard in the industry. If the market shifts—if the public decides that it prefers to eat out—then the company will have to shift or step around this potential problem into a new form of service to its customers if it wants to keep its position.

READING THE MARKET

Not all mine fields lie outside the company. In a small, Southern Illinois town, most of the restaurants are fast food American style places to eat. A man decided to come in, set up a lovely restaurant in the only high rise building in town. The view over the rolling plains was lovely, the setting charming, the prices upscale, and the success tremendous. This small town of 17,000 has continued to thrive even after the oil slump because it is also near many lakes and a great getaway resort for St. Louis. Money there was, interest there was, clients there were. Then why is it no longer there? Several people told us that the food quality began to slip. Why? Monopolies often forget that mediocre or inconsistent service and product [food] are still rejected even when you are the only show in town. Americans are too mobile and independent to accept a drop in quality or service.

Management and ownership changes can also make a major difference. Different priorities enter the picture, and unless one of those priorities is service/quality/commitment, then there will be a ripple effect downward throughout the entire organization. There may be sell-offs, cut-backs, staff reductions, etc. All of these can have negative impact and collectively they can spell disaster.

Turnover can also spell disaster. One major fast food chain has a 100% turnover in management. That means that there is not time to train these managers, and in turn the staff will be inadequately supervised and trained, too. How can there be consistent service and quality when there is not even consistency in staffing? There is no room in a success formula for excessive turnover.

Rapid growth can be a major problem. The best intentions in the world can go by the wayside as a company struggles to keep up with demand for which it is unprepared. One of our clients grew from a kitchen company in 1986 to a 1.2 million dollar company two years later. It had not laid a proper foundation, and although the product was great, the telephone order service wasn't, the delivery service back-logged (limited planning had been done for staffing), payment patterns to vendors were inconsistent, growth demanded about 50 new employees a month—ever try to find, screen, hire and train at that rate? The foundation for this growth wasn't in place, so the company could not keep its commitment—to its staff or customers. The result—bankruptcy.

MAKING A BAD JUDGMENT CALL

The government can plant a few mines, too. When taxes on services increase markedly companies tend to pass them on to their customers. For example, to cover the bed tax, hotels tend to increase the nightly rate. They may need to in order to maintain a logical profit margin, but a sharp jump may also cost them customers, the reduced customer base could result in staff reduction with a resultant drop in service or the quality of that service.

Sometimes production errors result in major problems. Think of what the consequences could be to a small company had it produced an automobile with faulty brakes which had to be recalled or had produced the pain relief bottles that were tampered with and poisoned.

Sometimes the failure to read the local market can pose problems. A grocery company opened with a splash in West Los Angeles in the mid-1980's. It was automated to the "Nth degree." You called in your order or drove up to an order window. They selected items from shelves, placed them on conveyer belts which delivered the items to a packaging point, and you could then pay and pick up your order. No walking up and down the aisles, no time wasted it you chose to call in, no energy depleted, and no trip to the store. It began with a splash and died without even a whimper. For one reason or another, the public wasn't ready or interested. Several factors may have entered into this failure, including

- Location: It was sited in an area catering heavily to singles who are pushed for time but are also finding that the aisles of the market are good places to meet people. In fact, several stores in that area have boosted their business markedly by publicizing singles nights.

- Many shoppers feel a need to "see" what they are going to buy.

- Many still comparison shop for price and convenience.

- Many still impulse buy—they haven't decided

what they want until they see it on the shelf.

- Many feel "out of control" when they can't make the choices.

Whatever the reason, the undertaking was poorly received. The market had not been studied sufficiently. In this case it was bad judgment, not bad luck, that caused the failure.

TRACKING

What most companies promise and say, outstanding companies do. Right now it is popular to talk about quality and service. Talk is not enough—as the old cliche goes, it is cheap. Action is needed!

Generate regular reports and statistics that will show how complaints are being handled, how many complaints are coming in and their focus. Seek information to determine customer views, attitudes, and opinions. Find out whether or not the customers have had their complaints resolved and **will** or **will not** return to **buy** the service or product again.

Consider this, if complaints drop it may not be that the problem is solved, it may just be that those who won't accept the quality or level product or service are going elsewhere. You won't know that until you ask.

Who should prepare these reports? The person or division with clout. When reports come from a power position they seem to have more impact. In addition, it is a good idea to have self-audits as well. Turn to the quality circle or focus groups to develop these self-audits. One of their strengths is the fact that the staff that prepares them is on-site. The problems aren't generic, they aren't industry or company-wide, they are their problems, at their site, and solutions should be in their hands.

Couple employee surveys, self-audits, and customer audits, and back them all up with **visible management.** You will then have the base for avoiding most of the problems. Visible management is not management that "takes over;" instead it is management that mingles with customers and employees and learns first hand what is happening. It is management that encourages dialogue, does not become defensive, and is familiar enough with the facility, service, and product to demonstrate concern, interest, and commitment.

MARKET RESEARCH—A NECESSITY

Market research is very important. How it is done varies, but some type of customer tracking system needs to be implemented.

LEARN FROM SUCCESS

> **"Every telephone call is extremely important to our club operation... The way we handle their call is most important, and in many cases the only contact we have with our member, which leaves a lasting impression of our company and operation. The telephone is a critical tool and must be used efficiently, especially in a service organization."**
>
> **Steve Zoumadukis**
> **President and CEO**
> **Automobile Club of Utah**

Polaroid operates an 800 number for customer assistance in five regional offices around the United States. It has used this approach for 13 years, and the front line representatives and their assistants handle telephone calls and consumer correspondence. About 1500 calls per day are handled, and about 40 percent of those are product questions, another 20 percent pre-purchase information requests, and only about 10 percent of the calls relate to service.

There are some very noteworthy aspects to this program.

- When lines into one area are busy, calls are off-loaded to insure prompt response.

- The number is put on the cameras and all literature, and customers are encouraged to call in questions or complaints.
- This service-driven company gives the representatives a great deal of authority to do whatever is needed to make the customer happy.
- The date of the customer's letter, not the date of receipt, is the date set as the base line. Thus the required time frame is dictated by the customer.
- Each caller is asked 6 questions—pre-developed to be used in relation to a particular camera. This data becomes part of the market research.
- This data is also used to identify and help identify root causes of problems.
- When representatives think they have solved the problem to the customer's satisfaction, they bring other products to the person's attention—thus cross selling.

Another industry giant, General Motors Corporation, adopted some very innovative approaches to problem prevention and complaint handling.

- Buick and Chevrolet used Core Groups to develop detailed recommendations with supporting program plans for increasing customer satisfaction.

- Chevrolet mounted an extensive research program to determine what women really wanted in their cars. Women are a major market, but had not been well researched before. To learn more about their buy choices, Chevrolet sponsored career success conferences and invited women in various regions to attend for a nominal fee plus their input on a questionnaire that provided the missing information.

Another giant, American Express Corporation has a number of autonomous divisions which could have a cross over in customer service. Because of this, they devised several approaches to facilitate rapid response to complaints and prevent future problems.

- They give an annual Great Performers Award to employees who provide customers with a high level of service (other companies do this as well—Epson America has Baccarat design a piece of crystal yearly for their awards, and those outstanding in service are given this one-time item—the mold is broken afterward).
- A toll-free number is printed on all bills.

The tracking system used by Northern Telecom, Inc. is outstanding and the heart of their problem-prevention efforts. They have three product-division specific questionnaires. The first focuses on sales and marketing services, delivery, installation, and repair. The second deals with product performance, and the third relates to key attributes of product use. Each survey is designed to determine the level of satisfaction and the probability of repurchase.

These simple reports provide vital data and pinpoint areas where action should be taken or efforts praised.

Retail stores are also concerned about tracking, and Neiman Marcus, a Dallas-based company, introduced two innovative problem-prevention approaches that seem to be working very well.

- Complex orders and their details are verified via a first class inquiry. If the information is not correct, the customer is asked to let them know by calling the 800 number given. When there is a peak mail period—like Christmas—mailgrams are used instead of first class mail.

- When the catalog item has any aspect which might trigger dissatisfaction—i.e., the color shown differs from the real color—the telephone representatives are briefed and instructed to provide information, advice, and help. This pre-planning and extra service has reduced returns and increased customer satisfaction.

Wouldn't it be great if we could end this chapter with a magic formula for success? Well, we can't, but it might help if you had some of the results of a national consumer survey. The report was issued on April 1, 1986, by the Technical Assistance Research Programs Institute at the request of the United States Office of Consumer Affairs which deals with consumer complaint handling in America. Every businessperson in the United States needs to be familiar with the results.

- 32.4% of households experienced a [consumer] problem.
- Many consumers who experience problems with products/services do not complain.
- Nearly 70% of those experiencing a problem did not complain.
- Fewer than 5% of the complaints about large ticket items ever reached the manufacturer.
- Those experiencing severe problems are more likely to complain than those experiencing minor ones.
- High income households are more likely to complain than low income ones.
- The young are more likely to complain than the elderly.

- People in the Northeastern part of the U.S. (particularly New York) report a disproportionately high complaint rate.
- There are three main reasons why people don't complain when dissatisfied:
  - it isn't worth the time or effort
  - they don't know how or where to go
  - they don't think it will do any good.

> **shared by Leon A. Gorman**
> **President**
> **L.L. Bean**
>
> **"A lot of people have fancy things to say about customer service, including me. But it's just a day-in, day-out ongoing, never-ending, unremitting, persevering, compassionate type of activity."**
>
> **from "Companies That Serve You Best" by Bro Uttal, FORTUNE, Dec. 7, 1987**

The study also showed that many are not satisfied with the action taken following the complaint, and the more severe the problem, the lower the level of customer satisfaction with the resolution. It was also learned that

- When there was potential financial loss of $1 - $5
  - and the complaint was satisfactorily resolved, 70% planned to repurchase.

  - and the complaint was unsatisfactorily resolved, only 46.2% would repurchase.
  - and the customer did not complain, only 36.8% would consider repurchasing.

- When the amount of potential loss was $100 or more
  - and the complaint was satisfactorily resolved 54.3% would repurchase.
  - and the complaint was not resolved only 19% would repurchase.
  - and the customer did not complain, only 9.5% would repurchase.

> **"Customer service results from superior product knowledge and service delivered with integrity and kindness."**
>
> **Jack E. Davis**
> **Manager**
> **Boy's Marine Market**

The study noted that by effectively soliciting and satisfying complaints, a company can actually generate profits. The study set forth a formula for determining the potential profit gain and that figure can then be calculated against the invested capital.

The successful management of change demands commitment, interest, attention, and a willingness to measure, evaluate, and take action. When those steps are in place, there is no reason for any company or organization to fear the marketplace, the minefields of competition will have been defused.

14

MOVING AHEAD OF THE COMPETITION

"The essence of customer service is simple. Treat the customer with respect, give him more than he expects, and make the experience of dealing with your company as easy as possible."

Paul B. Brown
"For Service Please Hold." Inc.
May 1989

In order to move ahead of your competition you need to provide the rewards—service, quality, style, support, etc.—that none of your competitors are offering.

- Find a need and fill it
- Find a problem and solve it
- Find a frustration and ease it.

Customers come to you for one of those three reasons, and the companies that meet those needs consistently, courteously, efficiently, and with quality are the ones to whom customers return.

> **"Sometimes we ask for six figure incomes out of our operations but forget the two figures—customer and employee—that make the six figures possible."**
>
> **Richard Bandley**
> **Owner/Manager**
> **Kentucky Fried Chicken**

You need three tools to mine the vein—eyes, ears, mouth. You need to listen to what people say they like, dislike, want and can't get. You need to read and note what is being said, and you need to talk about what you think you have found out and see if it is a discovery or a fantasy.

Let's look at some of the country's success stories—stories built on the three mining principles noted above.

- Have you ever used Liquid Paper? Some of us are even old enough to remember when secretaries used chalk to coat errors. To have a liquid coating that could blend in with the paper was a real blessing—particularly in the world before word processors or correction ribbons.

How did it come into being? One secretary who made errors, Bette Nesmith, created it for her own use, saw a demand grow, and was smart and daring enough to begin a business in her garage. That small venture begun in 1956 grew into the Nesmith Liquid Paper Corporation which Gillette bought in 1979 for $47.5 million.

- Post-Its is another success story. An accident that changed memo writing. One person working on a new glue product created a substance that wouldn't hold. He accidently found that he could put it on a piece of paper, stick the paper on something, and then peel it off again with no residue or discoloration problems. He started making his own little pads and soon the demand grew. Post-Its was a new product eagerly received by a world of note leavers.

What sets these people apart from the rest of us—we all make mistakes—is the fact that they acted on the positives that come from those errors. They created something that worked for them, and when they realized that it had market value, they **took action**! People say, "I thought of that years ago." That is probably so, but someone else acted.

Scott Cook, President and co-founder of Intuit Inc., believes that there are steps that can lead to that success. First, he isolates a task that everyone does on a regular basis and studies how they perform that task. He then asks as many people as possible what would make the job easier and uses this information to develop the product. He tests it on real users over and over, so when he delivers the product it is better than any competitors' and keeps copycats at bay.

> **"You've got to sell your competitive edge, whatever it is, and your presentations should emphasize the value of your advantages. Translating your key selling points into customer benefits creates sales."**
>
> **Ken Kisner**
> **Vice President/Sales**
> **Pulte Home Corporation of Texas**

DEFINE YOUR MARKET

It really doesn't matter what you do best or enjoy most if there are no customers for it. Often we become almost evangelical and want to "convert the world" to our system. Forget it. If they don't want it, they won't buy it! Find out what the market wants. Proctor and Gamble relied on this approach when they designed Pampers. Although they were not the first to market disposable diapers, they were the first to realize that parents didn't give "a hoot" about convenience, they wanted dry babies. By stressing absorbency and comfort, Proctor and Gamble turned Pampers into a market success because they responded to customer needs.

IMPROVE THE OLD

The Japanese have also moved into a power position in the world market by taking what is and refining it until it is markedly better than the original. There are some real advantages in just adding the new twist because

- people don't have to learn a new concept
- you have a base upon which to build
- you can see what is working and selling and why
- you can see what isn't working and isn't selling and determine why
- there is a market base already established
- time and up-front costs are far less
- most people don't miss what they never had, so marketing is more difficult when the concept or product is unknown, but relatively easy when an identified need is being met.

LISTEN TO YOUR CUSTOMERS

When 100 people are polled and 10 indicate an interest in the same thing or noted similar concerns, you have a trend or problem that needs consideration. When you spot a recurring interest or problem, take action.

PREPLAN AND PREPLAY

There are many exciting ideas—even great ideas—whose time has not yet come. Take care that you don't wade into water that is so deep that you sink. Take come precautions and

- Consider your plan and then preplay it in your mind. Remember the books on Inner Tennis and Inner Golf? They told the athletes to play through the entire game in their mind, and correct for errors before they ever went to the court or course. Learn from this—the system works. Take a step by step tour of what will have to be done if this idea or concept is to be marketed. It is far less costly to take these few minutes than it is to dash in, "do it" and lose your shirt and time if it doesn't work.

  - What pitfalls will you encounter?
  - What roadblocks?
  - What will you have to do,when, with whom, how?

- get input from others,

- Run a small scale test and find out what works, what needs to be done, what needs to be changed. Never invest more than 15 percent of your gross.

GET OFF THE FENCE

Once all systems are "go," get off the fence and take action. Many opportunities are lost while people sit and wonder if they should act. The formula is simple—listen, listen, listen, test, evaluate, and if all is still looking good, **ACT.**

REMEMBER—FAILURE CAN BE A STEPPING STONE TO SUCCESS

Don't be discouraged if every "great" idea doesn't pan out. It really doesn't change the fact that you are a winner when you do take that final step into the winner's circle.

COMPETITION GOES BEYOND PRODUCT

We hire lawyers to fight for us, we want parents to support us, and we want our doctor to care for us. Now let's put that same concept into the business world and have our company and its employees **support, care for,** and **fight for** the customer.

MAKE YOUR STAFF CUSTOMER ADVOCATES

If you want your staff to be the customers' advocate, then you have to make certain that the substructure is in place that will make it possible. We spoke earlier about the importance of market research—on-going market research—but that alone will not provide the needed foundation. There must be a mission statement that is more than words on paper.

> Long, short, witty, philosophical, it really doesn't matter. What does matter is that it specifically identifies your market, what you have to offer that market, and how you will approach that market. Your uniqueness—product, service, quality—needs to be noted as well.

The CEO of Metropolitan Life Insurance Company, John J. Creedon, says that MetLife has grown by building two ideas into its culture. First, a salesperson is responsible for everything that happens to one of his customers. Second, every MetLife employee is responsible to 'customers' within the company who depend on his service. Their mission is to "meet or exceed the expectations of the customer."

Like Creedon, you must build from your mission position a set of clearly defined guidelines that support your stated, publicized, corporate policies and principles. These principles must stress service and promote creative approaches to providing it. You need to be a customer advocate in a service-driven business.

"A goal without activity is like a destination without directions."

C. Louis Hohenstern
Management Consultant
Author

CUSTOMERS AND CUSTOMERS NEEDS

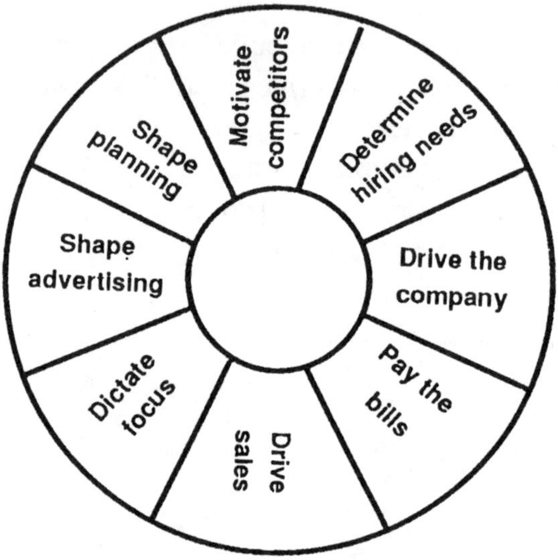

The competitive edge will automatically go to those who remember that customers deserve a quality package that meets their needs, so it is up to you to make certain that your company is customer-driven, not production-driven.

THE OLD FASHIONED IN THE NEW FASHIONED WORLD

"Put me first," is not a selfish plea from customers, it is a reasonable request since they are the reason your business exists. Take a look at how this attitude has changed and turn back the clock to improve the economic future and benefit the customer, too.

Look at medicine. The country doctor

- made house calls
- took time with each patient
- knew his patients by name and knew their families
- called to check on progress
- only over-booked when emergencies arose
- was active in his community
- was almost always respected
- was dedicated to service
- was affordable.

What has happened in the late twentieth century?

- There are more clinics.
- There are many HMO groups.
- Doctors rarely make house calls.
- Waiting is part of visiting the doctor.
- Fees are higher.
- Malpractice suits have increased. (Note: people seldom sue those they revere or who are friends.)

These changes mean that

- many doctors feel less satisfied by their career choice than earlier doctors did

- doctors feel greater stress
- doctors are more openly criticized
- expectations remain high but respect has dropped
- the cost of doing business has driven many out of the field or into HMO groups or clinics
- general satisfaction with medical treatment is lower
- people complain about fees but they don't realize how operating expenses (including insurance costs) have risen
- specialities and clinics or HMO treatment centers create situation where patients don't get to know the doctor and build rapport and trust.

Patients are customers and their dissatisfaction is going to reshape the medical profession. Change is needed if nationalized medicine is to stay at bay, and there is no reason why doctors and members of the medical profession can't bring about that change by looking at the problems that exist, the perceptions that are held, and the results they want and see how all of them can be brought into being. Some doctors and hospitals are already responding to their patients [customers] concerns and moving ahead of the competition.

- One doctor in Denver has adjusted his office hours so that patients who work can come in for evening appointments.

- One hospital is looking into using interns to make house calls.
- Several HMO groups are providing for house calls under certain circumstances.
- Large HMO groups are now shifting over to more personal attention—their advertising even stresses "your own doctor—someone who cares because he knows you."

Now there are still some areas that need dealing with, and others in the medical profession need to take note of the changes being made and their positive results in patient satisfaction.

Similar issues face many industries, and now the aging Baby Boomers are presenting another challenge. Many people—educators and business—aren't really looking at this market and its demographics. For generations we have had a youthful population, and industries and business geared up to meet its demands. Now, we have reached a point where by the year 2000, 40 to 45 million people will be over 65 (almost 20% of the population). In order to keep a competitive edge, industries and businesses must consider the consequences of this age shift. Ken Dychtwald points out in his book, AGE WAVE, that this group will

- own 77% of all financial assets in the U.S.
- purchase 43% of new domestic cars and 48% of the luxury cars
- purchase 80% of all luxury travel packages
- spend more than all other groups on health and personal care products
- eat out 3 times per week
- spend more per capita for groceries than other age groups
- buy 25% of all alcoholic beverages
- watch more television and read more newspapers than other age groups
- account for 40% of the total consumer demand.

Other markets are changing too. There is

- a larger singles market
- a large teen market
- increased mobility
- a relatively affluent customer base
- more women in the workforce
- increased dependance upon restaurants and fast food vendors
- fewer people willing to prepare food from "scratch"
- a drive to "stay young".

All of these trends impact heavily upon business. Look carefully at your own market, at the changes that are taking place, at the changes that will take place, and plan to take advantage of new markets, adjust for changes in old markets, and put greater emphasis upon meeting existing market needs. In other words, let your company be the baseline by which others in your industry are judged.

TOP SALES REWARDS from Burrell Colour

1. Announce the Employee's Name during a store meeting.
2. Post the Top Sales Person's Name on the bulletin board. (Even the smallest amount of recognition really boosts an Employee's ego, and SALES!)
3. Develop an "Employee of the Month" Program. Take their picture and keep it up on the bulletin board for a month.
4. Reward an Employee with a gift certificate or money.
5. Use gift certificates from other stores in your Mall. Examples:
   Free fries from the Hamburger Shop
   Free Hot Fudge Sundae
   $5.00 off a pair of Athletic shoes.
6. Lunch with the Manager!
7. Free Movie Passes.
8. Give a box of candy for a job well done!
9. Create a special parking spot for the Top Sales Person.
10. Ask your Vendors and Central Office for merchandise donations to use as prizes.
11. Minimize the store chores for the Top Sales Person.
12. Create a revolving award, like a trophy. The Top Sales Person keeps the trophy for a month.
13. Buy a Corsage. Have a morning meeting and pin it on the Top Achiever! Make a big deal about it! All day the Employee will be asked about her corsage!
14. If possible, give a paid day off!
15. Allow the Employee an extra break during the day.

APPENDIX A—SAMPLES

ATTENDANCE AWARD
from Burrell Colour

Employees who complete one month with a perfect attendance record are eligible for our attendance award. Perfect attendance shall also include not reporting to work late; or leaving before the end of your scheduled department hours.

There will be no exceptions for any reason. Absence from work, due to any reason, shall disqualify you for the month. Tardiness shall be counted as reporting late in the morning, exceeding the standard times established for department break and lunch periods, taking time off during scheduled work hours, or leaving work early. Lunch periods are not to exceed 30 minutes, except in the case of special events. During the year, if your department supervisor schedules a special event, such as our Christmas Buffets, during lunch hours, and verifies the extended time period for ALL department employees, the extended time will not count against your perfect attendance record. If you are on a scheduled vacation, that time will count toward perfect attendance.

At the end of each month, each eligible employee with a perfect attendance will receive an "ATTENDANCE AWARD COUPON." Employees with a six month consecutive perfect attendance will receive an additional "Bonus" coupon. An employee with a twelve month consecutive perfect attendance shall receive two additional "Bonus" coupons. These coupons will be accumulated, and used to purchase awards.

This program was instituted to show our appreciation to those employees who are on the job daily. We realize the efforts put forth by each of you; the loyalty shown to Burrell Colour and our customers, and the respect to your supervisor and co-workers by being here, on time, every day. This is an additional way for Burrell Colour to say "Thank You" for a job well done.

The Award List, showing the awards available and the number of coupons needed for each award, are shown on the following page.

Sample Award List from Burrell Colour

AWARD	# of Coupons
One week Caribbean Cruise for two, includes 3 day stay at Epcot Center (Disneyworld) free rental car, and $500 cash.	125
Trip for two to Hawaii, with $500 cash	100
IBM Personal Computer	100
Trip for two to Epcot Center (Disneyworld), for 4 days and 3 nights, plus $300 cash	50
Riding Lawn Mower	50
Stereo Equipment	50
Grandfather Clock	40
Sony 19: Color Television	30
Round-trip tickets for two—fly anywhere in the Continental United States. (You choose the destination, departure and return dates.)	30
Sony VCR	30
Lucien Piccard Men's Watch	20
Schwinn 10 Speed Bike	20
Gift Certificate to Service Merchandise	15
Portable 5" Color TV with AM/FM Radio	15
Weekend for two at the Hyatt Regency in Chicago	15

WHAT MYSTERY SHOPPERS LOOK AT

All retail evaluations should include the following areas:

- initial preparation (yellow page advertisement, etc)
- telephone techniques
- access
- signage for store
- quality of landscaping
- availability of parking condition
- outside facility appearance
- entrance/first impression
- ambiance: music, lighting, temperature, etc.
- floor organization
- display quality
- access—being about to find things
- supply for demand
- quality of merchandise
- pricing
- value
- cleanliness
  - store interior
  - restrooms
- company representatives:
  - appearance
  - professionalism
  - customer contact
  - speed of approach
  - friendliness
  - knowledge
  - helpfulness
  - salesmanship
  - quality of close

  - cash handling
- scenarios
- special services
- accuracy of advertising

These checkpoints were custom-designed to fit the retail industry. Similar custom-designed checklists are prepared for other industries or companies. For example, a checklist for an airline would include items such as:

- accuracy of fare and flight information
- whether or not one's frequent flyer number was noted or the program itself offered
- the efficiency of the transaction
- whether or not you were given information on ground transportation options.

On the other hand, the shopper would want to know if a bank employee:

- gave rates
- provided readily available data on competitive standing concerning yield, return, etc.

There is no one "blanket" assessment form that will provide the data needed. Instead, it is important to tailor each to the company and industry in order to maximize effectiveness, and that is what a good mystery shopping service does.

SEARCH FOR EXCELLENCE's Abbreviated Sample of a Face to Face QUICK SHOPPER FORM

Date:______ Arrival Time:________Departure:________

Name of Company: ______________________________

Location: ____________________________________

RATING SCALE

1	2	3	4	5
POOR	BELOW AVERAGE	AVERAGE	ABOVE AVERAGE	EXCELLENT

EXTERIOR:	RATING
1. Were the grounds clean, well kept and attractive?	1 2 3 4 5
2. Was the actual building clean and well kept?	1 2 3 4 5
3. Was the signage attractive and easily visible?	1 2 3 4 5

___ out of ____ = _____%

INTERIOR:	
1. Was the interior facility clean?	1 2 3 4 5
2. Was the ambiance comfortable? (Temperature, lighting, etc.)	1 2 3 4 5
3. Was the interior setting attractive/stylish?	1 2 3 4 5
4. Was the overall image projected one of quality?	1 2 3 4 5

___ out of ____ = _____%

CUSTOMER SERVICE:

1. Were personnel neat, clean and properly dressed?	1 2 3 4 5
2. Did staff appear eager, happy and well-adjusted?	1 2 3 4 5
3. Was the employee knowledgeable of products and price?	1 2 3 4 5
4. Did the employee have good sales abilities?	1 2 3 4 5
5. Did they handle the transaction efficiently?	1 2 3 4 5
6. Did they thank you or invite you back?	1 2 3 4 5

___ out of ____ = _____%

SEARCH FOR EXCELLENCE's
Abbreviated Sample of
TELEPHONE TECHNIQUES

Company Name: ____________________
Location called: ____________________
Company representative spoken to: ____________________
Length of call: ____________________

Comment on each section and score from 1 to 10.

RATING SCALE

1	3	5	7	10
EXTREMELY POOR	NEEDS IMPROVEMENT	AVERAGE	ABOVE AVERAGE	EXCELLENT

_____ 1. # of rings until the phone was answered:
1 ring = 10 points   2 rings = 9   3 rings = 8
4 rings = 5   5 rings = 2   6 rings + = 0

_____ 2. Greetings: How was and what was the greeting:

_____ 3. Hold transactions: Consider the length of hold and procedure used. (10 pts. if no hold time)

_____ 4. Professionalism of company representative:

_____ 5. Job/product knowledge:

_____ 6. Control of conversation:

_____ 7. Salesmanship of product/company:

SEARCH FOR EXCELLENCE's

Abbreviated Sample of a FAST FOOD ESTABLISHMENT

Circle one. Y= yes N = No NA = Not available

G. DRIVE UP TO WINDOW

Y N NA 1. Was the drive thru lane easy to maneuver through?
Y N NA 2. Was the building itself in this area spotless?
Y N NA 3. Was the shrubbery free of trash, cigarettes...?
Y N NA 4. Was the drive thru lane free of trash,...?
Y N NA 5. Were directional arrows properly placed?
Y N NA 6. Could you easily distinguish where to pick up the order?
Y N NA 7. Cold you easily distinguish where to pay for the order?

Comments/suggestions:

I. PICK UP WINDOW/COMPANY REPRESENTATIVE

What was the greeting?:"________________________________"
Y N NA 1. Was the greeting professional?
Y N NA 2. Friendly?
Y N NA 3. Did they smile?
Y N NA 4. Was the window clean?
Y N NA 5. Was their immediate work are neat and clean?
Y N NA 6. Did they repeat the amount of your bill?
Y N NA 7. Did they say please?
Y N NA 8. Did they count back your change to you?
Y N NA 9. Did they say thank you?
Y N NA 10. Did they appear to know how to handle cash?
Y N NA 11. Did they suggest that you enjoy your meal?
Y N NA 12. Was your meal ready when you arrived at the window?
If you had to wait for your order, how long?_____
Y N NA 13. Did you consider this wait an acceptable amount of time?
Y N NA 14. Did you receive the proper order?

SEARCH FOR EXCELLENCE's Example of a Face-to-Face Assessment

Narrative Summary

***Restaurant: Weekend Shop

Date: 4/8/89
Entered: 7:55 p.m.
Exited: 9:45 p.m.

When we drove toward the restaurant, we saw the lighted temporary sign from a far distance away. Although the sign was eye catching, I feel a nice wood carved or "theme-type" replica sign would be much more attractive. As we pulled in, we smelled the delicious aroma of steaks cooking. The parking lot had many large potholes and was very full.

When we walked into the lobby, there were many people sitting against the wall on the wooden benches. At first, we were set back, wondering how long we would need to wait. We stood by the door, wondering if one of the people in the room was a host. I started to walk toward the entrance to the restaurant, but was concerned that I might upset the waiting customers, if they were in some type of line.

Finally, the host asked, "How many?" and type of

smoking preference. I asked the wait time and he quoted 40 minutes. Had we not been there on assignment, I think we would have left and gone elsewhere due to the wait. (I was surprised later, when we were seated, at the number of empty seats in the restaurant. I believe that all of the waiting customers could have been seated throughout the empty seats.)

Since we were waiting, we decided to go to the rest room. Inside the restaurant, the atmosphere seemed very upbeat and fun. The restrooms were satisfactory, however I feel they could be much cleaner, considering the establishment is a restaurant. (When I returned later, they had not been serviced and were in much worse condition.)

When we went back into the lobby, it seemed very boring and even depressing. Walking into the lobby from the restaurant was almost a culture-shock. There was no music in the lobby...just silence and people sitting, staring across the small room at each other. It almost felt like torture or a doctor's office. The host appeared even more bored than the waiting customers. He did not try to make conversation or ease the pain of waiting in the small, dark room.

On seven occasions, potential customers opened the exterior door to the lobby. Once they looked inside, they gasped at the wait and saw the many heads who turned to look at them. Two of the customers did not even set foot inside, they just closed the door. The others came inside and asked the wait time. Two of the groups decided to stay and three left. I think that, had the host been a little more outgoing or cajoled them into staying, they all would have waited.

As a non-smoker, I was surprised that there was no smoking control over the lobby. There is absolutely no ventilation in the small, wooden room. After waiting 30 minutes, the room became foggy and filled with smoke. I do not believe there are ashtrays in the room either, so cigarette butts were on the floor.

As we waited, I liked how they served beverages and cocktails to waiting customers. There was one waitress taking care of orders (female, blonde, young 20's). Considering the large amount of waiting customers, she did her job quite well and was courteous. She was sure to receive payment for each order, before moving on to the next customer.

I was pleased that our name was called in 30 minutes, after the wait was quoted at 40 minutes. The hostess walked in front of us to the table, but did not say anything to us. We walked briskly in order to keep up with her. She seemed like she would be a nice person if she would have spoken. However, she smiled and directed us to our seats without saying a word.

When our server arrived, she was pleasant upon first impression. She asked if we wanted drinks, then asked about an appetizer by naming a few off the menu. We ordered cheese sticks and fried mushrooms, as well as the remainder of our entree. The waitress asked if we wanted a baked potato to go with the meal, but did not explain that there was an extra charge. She was very nice while taking the order.

We asked the waitress' name and it was "*****". When she brought our steaks, she asked which one of us had the rare and which had the medium. After we cut into the steaks and ate a few bites, we realized she had reversed the two steaks and so we traded the partially eaten steaks across the table. We did not get any condiments with our steaks when the steaks arrived. It took 4-5 minutes to get our potatoes and 12 to get our beans. ***** did not apologize for the delay, she just put the items on the table and walked away.

As we ate our meal, the crowd in the restaurant slowly diminished. Our service also diminished as it got slower in the restaurant. The staff started to gather at the wait stations to chat. We had quite a few empty dishes and had to ask that they be removed, when it was obvious they were cluttering the table. At this point, ***** offered additional beans. (Why are the beans not served in individual dishes instead of the one large bowl? This would be our preference.)

The way our table was arranged, we could see behind the bar. One of the managers (male, 6' 0", dark hair, red plaid shirt) consistently went behind the bar to drink from a plastic mixer bottle. The liquid appeared to be a sweet and sour or margarita mix. I thought it unusual he would drink directly from the bottle in public. He also came from the back numerous times, snacking on food.

After we were finished eating, we waited for a long time to get our check and dessert. I was pleased that the bar was stocked with a particular liqueur, which some restaurants do not stock.

We made friends with the couple next to us, who were frequent customers. As with our experience, ***** initially provided great service for the customers next to us...it was almost as if she lost interest with each of us; our transactions were one hour apart.

Overall, we enjoyed our meal. Having been to the Dallas restaurant, I believe I prefer the Dallas location. I truly enjoy the concept of the restaurant, one that you have to "be in the mood for". The noise level seemed very loud, perhaps hindering *****'s ability to provide the service one expects at a steak dinner.

I will definitely return to ***Restaurant, as we usually do when "tourists" are in town. However, I may be more concerned about the service we will receive, after this average to below-average experience.

WELCOME TO NORDSTROM

We're glad to have you with our Company

Our number one goal is to provide outstanding customer service

Set both your personal and professional goals high

We have great confidence in your ability to achieve them.

NORDSTROM RULES

RULE #1: Use your good judgment in all situations

There will be no additional rules.

Please feel free to ask your department manager, store manager, or division general manager any question at any time.

NORDSTROM

CUSTOMER SERVICE PROGRAM
Before & After Training and Incentives
Conducted by SEARCH FOR EXCELLENCE, INC.

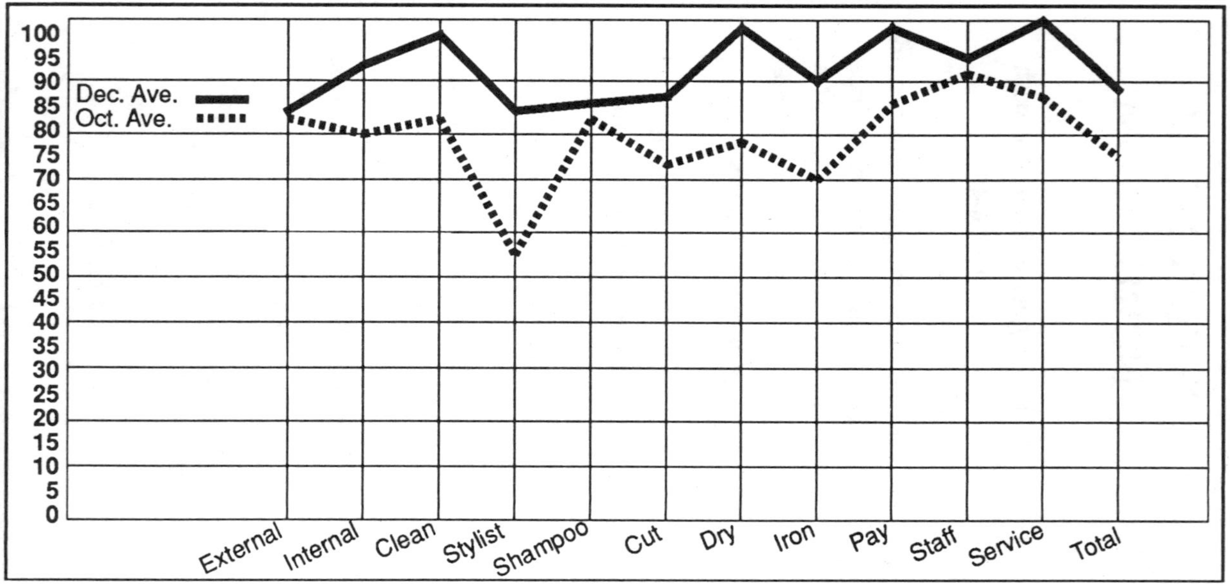

TRAITS OF BEHAVIORAL STYLES

LEADERS

You enjoy being in a position of control and find that slow moving activities bore or frustrate you. In addition to being ambitious, you are also quite positive about your own ability. Your dress is generally "power dress" or corporate attire and the look is "old money." Your communication style is straightforward, direct, decisive, and at times, even blunt. You are resourceful, enjoy a challenge and are result-oriented. You speak rapidly, speed up when you get excited and you are competitive.

PERSUADERS

You are friendly, outgoing, sociable and enthusiastic. You prefer a setting which is colorful, warm and filled with plants and pictures of living things. Your dress is stylish and coordinated, and your speech is persuasive and filled with images. You are optimistic and want to please and help others. Details bore you, but people never do. It would not be surprising to find that you impluse-buy and enjoy objects which others consider status symbols.

PATIENT PERSON

Your speech is measured and controlled, and in all probability, your career choice required that you specialize in depth. You are conservative, fashionable, and your attire is always understated. Family is very important to you, and it is important that your home have space for family gatherings. You may well have projects underway and collections on display in your home, and you most likely live in a stable, well-established neighborhood. Change is something you prefer to avoid, but traditions are important to keep. You must know all the facts before you make a decision, since you want to be "sure."

CAREFUL PERSON

You are good at precision work and details and you need to know "why." Rules, regulations, and traditions are followed by you, and you are truly conscientious. Your dress is neat, subdued, and generally well-coordinated. Although you are open-minded, you are very conservative—even negative—when it comes to change. You are frugal, want detailed information, but always ask for it in a very diplomatic manner. In your world, there is a place for everything and everything is in its place. Order is important to you, as is a good return on your dollar.

RESERVED PERSON

Because you are shy, others may feel you are suspicious or aloof; in part this may be because you are "turned off" by excessive emotionalism or "glad-handing." You are not overly concerned about clothes, but you do enjoy the latest gadgets, and security is important. Facts are the basis of all decisions, as far as you are concerned, and you make your decisions only after careful analysis. You have a few very close friends, but are not what is termed a "social being." You enjoy working with ideas and concepts and do so without being part of a multi-person environment. You are not one to waste time on small talk.

INDEPENDENT PERSON

You are not interested in details, are bored by them in fact, and you question the establishment. Others see you as a nonconformist who enjoys the role of maverick. You are highly independent, see the big picture, love a challenge, are open to new ideas and may even be a risk-taker. You enjoy the adversarial role, hate any attempt to control you and find a good argument stimulating. Freedom and excitement are important, and you hate people who complicate issues, dwell on details, or waste time.

Manage—Compete—Succeed

(Check each service requested)

PROFESSIONAL MYSTERY SHOPPING SERVICES

- ❑ **CUSTOMER SERVICE:** Acquire first-hand, data on employee courtesy, selling skills, product knowledge, and your customer's overall experience.
- ❑ **TELEPHONE TECHNIQUES:** Uncovers valuable information on your company's telephone image and selling techniques.
- ❑ **BRANCH/FRANCHISE COMPLIANCE:** Determines branch-wide or system-wide customer service consistency and compliance to standards.
- ❑ **PROMOTIONAL SUPPORT:** Ensures participation in your consumer promotions and compliance with policy.
- ❑ **COMPETITOR STUDIES:** Investigates the quality of customer service offered by your competitors. Vital strategic planning information.
- ❑ **COMMENT CARD SERVICES:** Gathers information from your current customers. Cards designed to meet your feedback objectives. Cumulative trends are highlighted. Weekly, bi-weekly, or monthly reports.

APPENDIX B—PRODUCTS /SERVICES

TRAINING AND CONSULTING SERVICES

- ❑ **QUICK CHECK:** A means of identifying individual drive, compliance, pace, and interaction levels as well as stress and pressures.
- ❑ **JOB CHECK:** Identifies the behaviors needed for success in a given position.
- ❑ **VALUES CHECK:** Identifies the motivators that make it possible to build individualized motivational packages.
- ❑ **BRAIN CHECK:** Identifying dominance patterns which when coupled with other data makes it possible to increase productivity.
- ❑ **TRAINING:** Management, customer service, sales training custom tailored to your needs.
- ❑ **STRATEGY FOCUS SESSIONS:** Make it possible to identify, focus, and design solutions to problems or approaches to meeting goals quickly and effectively. One session can produce a detailed plan of action.

BOOKS

EVERYONE IS A CUSTOMER: Practical, easy to read—the "one minute manager of customer relations." **$12.95**

PEOPLE POWER: An easy to follow guide to effective communication and people management. **$12.95**

CUSTOMERS RUN YOUR COMPANY: THEY PAY THE BILLS: Tips for shaping and running a service-driven company in order to hold your own or even expand your share of the marketplace. **$12.95**

ORDER BLANK

Return to: Kearney/Bandley Enterprises
563 Washington Street, Marina del Rey, CA 90291
Call (213) 822-3751

OR

Search for Excellence
2100 Highway 360, Suite 200B
Grand Prairie, TX 75050
(214) 988-0099

NAME: ____________________
TITLE: ____________________
COMPANY: ____________________
ADDRESS: ____________________
CITY: ____________________ **STATE:** ________ **ZIP:** __________

Services/Products/Quantity:

____
____
____
____
____
____

California residents add 6.5% sales tax ____________
Postage/Handling 5% ____________
Total ____________

Check enclosed: # ____________________
Bill to my VISA ____________ MasterCard ____________
Card #: ____________________
Expiration Date: ____________________
Signature: ____________________